A TIPPY CANOE
and CANADA TOO

An Adventure in
Animal Antics and Wilderness Wisdom

by

SAM CAMPBELL
The Philosopher of the Forest

CONTENTS

I	Blue Note in a Sylvan Symphony	11
II	Digging Up a Dream	20
III	The Double Cross—and Still-Mo	29
IV	Six Little Sausages	35
V	A Canoe and a Quandary	40
VI	A Lisp Along a Forest Trail	43
VII	Super-Sense and Non-Sense	56
VIII	A Porky Problem and Hi-Bub	61
IX	Racket from Solitude	69
X	A Goad from Sandy	77
XI	Blessed Noothanth	81
XII	Ratzy-Watzy	92
XIII	Horizons and Hopes	104
XIV	Inky!	112
XV	A Tent for Two	121
XVI	A Dream That Wouldn't Stay Put	131
XVII	Carrots and Comics	141
XVIII	When Soul Sings	152
XIX	A Dream Comes True	157
XX	Threshold of the Wilderness	167
XXI	Challenge in the Wilderness	179
XXII	Beauty and a Beast	190
XXIII	Waves and Woes	197
XXIV	Busy Beavers of Maybe Lake	203
XXV	The Guitar Makes a Conquest	211
XXVI	The Secret of Indian Joe	220
XXVII	Memories and Manna	233
XXVIII	A Canoe in the Skies	242

I

BLUE NOTE IN A SYLVAN SYMPHONY

GINY and I sang as we followed the winding course of our forest road. We were homeward bound! Yet a few miles and we would reach that little cabin set like a jewel on an island, centering the life-teeming forest of northern Wisconsin.

Our song—whether music critics would approve of it or not—gave vent to our feelings. It expressed what we wished to say to ourselves and for ourselves. Through the years we had sung it beside campfires, or as we drifted in a canoe along remote silent shores. In cities we had used it to lift our thoughts above urban confusion. We sang it during difficulties to foster faith. And now its words were being lived again:

> I know a land that holds our treasure,
> Where blessings flow forth without measure,
> Far from all turmoil and aimless strife,
> Where all nature sings with life.
>
> I know a road that winds and winds
> Through cooling woods of towering pines,
> That scent each breeze with fragrance rare,
> And sweet bird songs fill the air.
>
> From the end of the road a trail leads on
> Beyond where the woodsman's ax has gone,
> Through verdant halls where the wild life roams
> And shadows hide elves and gnomes.

At the end of the trail is a wooded lake
So cool and clear where the shy deer take
Their fill in the night when the wide world sleeps
And darkness their secret keeps.

On the shore of the lake is an old camp ground,
In its quiet and peace our treasure's found.
Here God is so near, here doth love prevail
In that camp on a lake, over road and trail.

This song was written when the going to our Sanctuary was fraught with problems and savored of adventure. No cabin awaited us then. The tent we carried on our backs was our dwelling, and the packsacks we tugged and lifted bore our supplies. The coming of conveniences had only deepened our devotion to our forest haven, so that the sentiment of our song held true. Travel had become easier, roads came closer, a cabin had replaced a tent, yet "Here God is so near, here doth love prevail."

We had reached the road's end. By way of greeting to the region we walked down to the lake shore, looked out to distant pine-covered hills, and dipped our fingers in the waters to shake hands with incoming wavelets. From this point we must travel by water a slight two miles.

Anxious to close the last gap separating us from our Sanctuary, we opened a little shed which stands at the road's end, and brought out our old canoe. It was then that the smiles died temporarily from our lips. The old canoe was in deplorable condition! When I took hold of the railing to lift it, slivers of rotted wood came out in my hand. There was a crack high in the side through which I could see daylight. The bottom was warped with potential breaks. Decay was appearing at many vital spots. Some repair work might delay the day of final destruction, but there was too little to build on to have the work last long. "Buddie," as we had named this grand old craft, was nearing the end of its service.

Giny and I had known when we stored the canoe away the previous autumn that it was in bad shape. Winter cold had deepened all scars. Buddie was a veneer canoe, made of two layers of birch and an inner layer of cedar. Finished with clear varnish so that the natural beauty of the wood was revealed, it looked like the featherweight birchbark canoes made by Indians and pioneers. The strength of the craft was as amazing as its lightness and maneuverability. Through the years it had carried loads and withstood strains that would have been fatal to any craft of less stability. But now the veneer was parting in a dozen places, braces were crumbling, and the sides separating from railings.

"Poor old Buddie!" I said, patting the canoe affectionately.

"Will it get us over to the Sanctuary?" Giny asked.

I nodded. There was still some service in the old craft. It wasn't our immediate convenience that concerned me. I was faced with losing a pal, a companion. No doubt it is silly to become so attached to an inanimate thing. Yet any real, paddle-swinging, packsack-toting canoeist would understand.

Buddie had shared many of our adventures. I knew

just what to expect from it, knew when to apply the stroke, when to back water, knew just what response I would get. I knew just how it would ride high waves, or skim through fast rapids. There had been times when it was my only companion for days of wilderness travel. It had been a true partnership affair. It had carried me across the lakes, I had carried it across portages. Often the old craft turned upside down on a shore had been my only shelter. Sometimes when we have reached the down end of a bad rapids or the lee side of a rough lake I have patted the side of the faithful old canoe and said, "Well done, Buddie—thanks a million!"

"Maybe we won't have to give it up right away," Giny was saying, with her usual hopefulness. "We could use it through this season when the lake is quiet—wear life jackets if necessary."

Now that is what I mean by a true canoe lover! Giny is one of the best. It would have been neither a great expense nor much difficulty to buy another canoe. Besides, we had another one which we seldom used. Any one without sentiment would have said, "All right, the old boat is finished! That gives us some fine kindling wood." Not Giny!

We picked up the light craft and carried it to the lake shore, Giny at one end, I at the other. Here in better light we examined it more closely. The pattern of disintegration was plain.

We fell to looking and laughing at the many marks and scars. It was like reading an old diary. Across the bottom were four long parallel scratches indented into the wood, plainly visible though varnished over. It was the autograph left by Bunny Hunch and Big Boy, our pet bear cubs, that day years ago when I took them for a ride. I should say, when I started to take them for a ride, for we had hardly gone ten feet before they tipped us over, scratching this record in the canoe as they did so.

There were other deep indentations along the railings, as though done with a chisel. This was the work of our porcupines, old Inky, and the more recent two, Salt and Pepper. The varnish was much to their liking, but unable to make so delicate a bite they had taken some of the wood, too. Toward the bow was some green paint, also deep under coats of varnish. Rack and Ruin, the raccoons, had done that by dipping their ever-inquisitive front feet in a can of paint and then trailing across the canoe. I could have sandpapered it off, but I never wanted to. Then there were dainty little marks along the edge of the seats. These spoke of the days when our five red squirrels, Eeny, Meeny, Miney, Mo and Still-Mo, were developing their teeth. And what could be better for incisors, molars and such things than to nibble on the crisp veneer of that canoe?

Then there was the "wound stripe," as I referred to a large square patch in Buddie's bow. A thin copper plate had been bolted and glued in place, in color a sharp contrast to the rest of the canoe. One uninformed might have thought it somewhat marred the beauty of the craft, but to us who knew the story it was a badge of honor. I recall the day very vividly, still with a shudder. I was out in the canoe, just idly cruising the shores. The lake was calm and a peaceful dusk was settling on the landscape. I rounded a little point, and saw some distance ahead an outboard motorboat, in which a boy was laboring to get the engine started. Outboard motors did not behave so well in those days. There were a lot of little frailties which kept them from starting at the right time and sometimes stopped them at the wrong time. The boy was becoming quite impatient. No doubt he had been cranking futilely for a half hour or more. As I watched him, he stood up to give the starter rope a harder jerk. The engine suddenly started off at terrific speed, the boat shot forward, and the boy, losing his balance, plunged over the side. He could swim well, but this offered him little safety. The boat, running wildly without a pilot, was circling about, its motor snarling like some vicious beast bent on destruction. Twice it passed near the swimmer, its fiercely whirling propeller blades churning the water but a few inches from him.

Fear gripped me for a moment. It seemed the distance involved and the circumstances would make it impossible to get to the boy in time! I remember saying aloud then to the old canoe, "Buddie, we can do it! The strength of God is on our side." I lunged forward to the center of the canoe on my knees, dipped my paddle in and stroked as I never had before. How Buddie responded!

The boat passed the boy again, this time actually touching him. Buddie and I were nearing rapidly. There was only one thing to do. "Buddie, you have to take it!" I called, as I gave the stroke that sent the craft right into the path of the boat. There was a sickening crash as the motorboat struck us. Slivers from Buddie's bow sprayed across the surface of the water. It was only a moment's delay in the frantic flight of the heavier craft, but enough to permit me to pull myself within reach of the motor and shut it off.

With the snarl taken out of the air, the habitual quiet of the region seemed deeper than ever. The boy swam over and climbed into his boat. I sat looking at the gaping hole in my canoe. The wound was rather high on the side, and by shifting my weight I kept it from taking in lake water. The boy was as sorry for the damage done the canoe as he was grateful for his rescue.

"Never mind, lad," I said. "We will patch Buddie some way. Only the best canoe in the world could have done what this one did today. We'll be proud of that scar."

Giny was thinking of this as she ran her fingers over the copper plate, searching for breaks in the seam. In a moment she looked up at me, smiling. "There are other markings on Buddie that do not show so plainly, but they are surely there," she said. Giny can never remain melancholy long. "There are the imprint of starlight, the blush of dawns and sunsets, and the autograph of wavelets. . . ."

"And the polishing done by moonbeams and the fingerprints of dew!" I added, my mood brightening.

As we loaded our equipment into the old canoe, we became happier, remembering the thousand and one nights and days we had spent in it. There must be somewhere between bow and stern the written record of northern lights whose gentle beams had caressed its sides. Somewhere and in some way it bore record of meteors streaking the skies, of the coyote's cry, of the soft whir of wings as the owl passed, of the beaver splash and the great buck posing in the moonlight.

We launched out into the lake and paddled through the winding channel leading to our Sanctuary. A tiny trickle of water found its way through a scar in the canoe bow. It flowed ominously past Giny's feet as she moved out of its way. "That isn't so much!" she commented, though she eyed the leak regretfully.

We paused in our stroking and laid our paddles across our knees to note the smoothness and silence of our old craft. It seemed much the same as it always had, except for the trickle that flowed on. There was truly magic about Buddie. A muskrat was seen swimming across the channel, and so quietly did we approach him that he did not detect us until we were within reach of him. Then he dived to obscurity. An old blue heron was pacing along the shore in measured strides. We drifted to within a few feet of him before he gave his loud alarming squawk and took awkwardly to air.

"Buddie, you still have your old charm," said Giny, patting the canoe. "I'll predict we have a lot more adventures together, before we give you up."

II

DIGGING UP A DREAM

THE day of our arrival was the sort in which hurry does not fit. Water kept coming in through the leak in Buddie's bow until a sizable puddle swished about on the bottom. We shuffled the baggage, protecting the more delicate things—and just let it swish!

That romantic, lazy warmth of spring was in the air. Nature didn't want to go anywhere or do anything in particular. She just wanted to lie in the sunshine on the hillsides, fan herself with an occasional breeze and let fancy take its course. We were infected with the mood. We slowly zigzagged our way toward the island, paddling almost without purpose. Everything in the forest world was so drowsy it seemed to be walking in its sleep.

"There is a dream engraved somewhere on the hull of this canoe—remember?" Giny asked—a question in keeping with the hour.

"A dream, dear?" I reflected for a moment, but did not catch the theme.

"Yes, a dream we had four years ago, together with Sandy the Squoip. Now do you recollect it?"

"Why, yes—surely I remember." I chuckled. "Sandy! Funny old Sandy the Squoip! How he loved Buddie! The boy just lived on plans that never got out of the dream stage. I wonder where he is now."

By comments we pieced our recollection together. Sandy the Squoip was a perfectly silly nickname that got attached to one of our young friends during his brief visit to our Sanuctuary in the spring of 1941. He was eighteen at the time, and adept at foolishness. It all arose out of a series of gags, introduced by the boy himself. It was a dialogue. With both my dignity and sanity affected by the spell of the northwoods, I co-operated with him. Sandy—six feet tall, slender, muscular, and crowned with wavy light-colored hair of Scandinavian origin—would assume the attitude and culture of a Boweryite.

"Say, guy!" he would drawl at me.

This was my cue to abandon all semblance of intelligence, and answer in an innocent and superior tone, "Yes?" Then the thoroughly inane repartee went something like this:

He: "I saw a boid tudday, up'na tree."

I: "You don't mean a *boid,* my friend, you mean a *bird.*"

He: "Huh? Well —it choiped like a boid, and it was after a woim."

I: "No—not a *woim,* you mean a *worm.*"

He: "Huh? But it squoimed like a woim, and it was inna doit."

I: "Not *doit*—no, you mean *dirt!*"

He: "Well, it looked like doit, and it *choimed like a squoip.*"

Don't try to make anything out of that last sentence. It is devoid of significance or the slightest suggestion of meaning. Sandy called it "the supreme goat-getter"—because Giny simply couldn't stand it. When he reached this climax, usually we went running out the cabin doors for dear life, mops, brooms, frying pans or whatever Giny could lay her hands on coming after us with rather good aim.

Soon the coined word "Squoip" became fixed to our northwoods vocabulary, signifying anything or anyone altogether lacking in sanity. A Squoip was four degrees lower than a nitwit. And for his part in introducing this idiocy into the Sanctuary vernacular—already having more than its share of crazy traditions and customs—our young friend was officially named "The Squoip."

It is proverbial that a rich man can afford to wear rags. For similar reason, our sandy-haired lad could well afford the uncomplimentary insinuation of his nickname. He had a most appealing personality and was rich in ability and accomplishments. His record through high school had been splendid.

We remembered well how he looked in those early teen years, already manly but retaining the lighthearted joy of youth. His smile was so near the surface that it was breaking through all the time, in his eyes, on his lips, in his cheery attitude, in his strong hand clasp. Sandy's nose was a little crooked. That was a reminder of the time he won an inter-scholastic wrestling title. It had been twisted a little more during a hard-fought football game. But you never felt that his strength was a threat to anyone. He was one of the most unchallenging people I have ever known. His easy manners made everyone in his company feel free, and at the same time all who met him knew he couldn't be pushed around.

Sandy had a problem. It became more and more heavy upon his shoulders as high school years drew to a close. In spite of his fine record, he had a growing feeling that he was a misfit. His companions were heading for clearly defined objectives. One was going to a certain college for training in architecture, another chose civil engineering, another electrical engineering, another prepared for a business course. But Sandy rebelled at such prospects and he couldn't understand why. He really desired success. He wanted his parents to be proud of him. But cities and commercial careers irked him deeply.

His home was a northern Minnesota town. Here he could enter the great canoe wilderness areas of the United States and Canada quickly. From the moment he did, the world sparkled with joy and purpose. It was hard labor to lift a pen for an English composition, but he could carry an eighty-pound pack and a ninety-pound canoe without a grunt! There seemed to be little or no reason for the tricks of trigonometry, but figuring out his way through the wilderness and living by the cleverness of woodcraft—that was vastly important. It was no light problem for Sandy. He feared he was a failure, and that is the greatest fear that ever assails human thought.

Sandy had about decided to smother all his natural inclinations, and force himself through an orthodox career. He would take up some standard training—any kind, it didn't make much difference which—and live in a way that would avoid the world's laughter and criticism.

Then the planning of his immediate experience was taken from him. He, and thousands of others like him, were drawn into military service—to be ready for something everyone hoped would never happen.

Sandy visited us on a furlough soon after he had been inducted into military service. His time was short, but sufficient for him to fall in love with our Sanctuary, our animal friends and particularly with Buddie the canoe.

Sandy was a thoroughbred canoeist. He could handle bow paddle or stern with the best of them, and he knew the sentimental side of canoe lore too. He admired the way Buddie was formed, the way it lifted and balanced on his shoulders, the way it handled in the water. Every possible hour of his stay was spent in or with our canoe.

"I want to see how old Buddie would look in that Canadian country!" he exclaimed, his eyes kindled with that grand enthusiasm with which he was blessed. "Just fancy that shapely hull beneath the picture rocks of Lac La Croix or in the narrows of Agnes Lake!" Then with an explosive "Oh, boy!" he brought a fist against the palm of his other hand in a gesture that spoke volumes.

Such enthusiasm brings about its own demonstration. I was talking to the lad with serious purpose before I realized it. "Sandy, did you ever come across a little wilderness lake, well off the main traveled canoe routes, deep in game country, where we might go to study animals and not be disturbed by other travelers?"

Sandy the Squoip nearly popped with excitement. "Yes, I have—er, no I haven't," he stammered, sensing the reason for the question and afraid he might say the wrong thing. "That is, I know of little lakes that have no names and no trails. Why? What are we going to do?" He was on his feet standing before me, animated as if he expected to start that minute.

"Take it easy, you Squoip," I laughed, trying to be calm but with only partial success. "You see, Giny and I need to find such a little lake where we may carry on studies which are no longer easy here. We love this spot, and it will always be our home, but more and more people are coming into this region. As you know, when people come in animals either go out or change their habits in some ways. Especially do we have a problem in working with larger animals now—such as bear, wildcats and wolves. So we have our dream in which there is a lake already named—*Sanctuary Lake.* We have never seen it, don't know just where to look for it, in fact don't really know if such a place exists—but we dream anyway. If we ever found it we would go to it for part of each season to work at those things we cannot do here. Sanctuary Lake would have to be small so we could go out in all kinds of weather. It would have high land and low land and be marked with great animal runaways."

To give Sandy an idea like that is like tossing gasoline on a fire. In an instant he was aflame with enthusiasm. "It would have a little stream running through an aspen forest, for beaver!" he joined in, taking the subject right away from me. "There would be an eagle's nest on one shore and an osprey's too. I'll bet our camp would be in a great stand of virgin red pines. There would be cedar swamps for deer in winter, lily pads along the shore to draw moose, berry patches for bears—— Oh, boy, when do we start?"

"Easy Sandy, easy!" I laughed. "This is only a dream. If you make so much noise you may wake us up. Have you forgotten about the army?"

"No—but part of me is going to stay in that dream!"

said Sandy, his enthusiasm unabated. "I have to find Sanctuary Lake. What a trip for Buddie. We are going to make this dream come true. I'll be through with the army in a year. Then can we go?"

The promise was made, though my hopes dared not picture his return from the army in a year, or in two years. Intuitively we knew what was before us.

But Sandy the Squoip was irrepressible. As he bade us good-by at the end of his furlough, he stooped down and patted the old canoe. "Buddie, you and I have a date—a year from now," he said confidently.

A year from then Sandy was undergoing special and strenuous training high in our Western mountains. The Pearl Harbor attack had pulled our heads out of the sands and we realized we were at war. Another year passed and our lad was on his way for the great test. When last heard from he was fighting in the mountains of northern Italy. There were promotions. There was a citation for bravery. Then there were months during which we heard nothing from or of our Sandy. VE Day had come and guns were silenced in half the world.

"But we are going to hear from him," said Giny confidently, as we sculled along, now nearing our island. "I just know Sandy is all right. If nothing else would carry him through, the desire to find Sanctuary Lake would bring him back. Only now—" she lifted her feet which were dripping with the water we had taken in—"I am afraid Buddie will never carry out his part of the dream. What do you think?"

"I'll be satisfied if we just get up to that shore before we swamp," I replied, my skepticism aggravated by the waves that were washing up my trouser legs.

There had been a canoe song written about our planned search for Sanctuary Lake. It was to the melody of the Marines' Hymn which gives as fine a rhythm for paddling as it does for marching. We recalled it now, and sang it to quicken our pace before calamity overtook us.

> Up along the north horizon,
> Where Aurora's searchlights play,
> There's a lake that rests in solitude
> And the wildwood chants its lay.
> In the land of bears and beavers,
> In the haunt of doe and fawn,
> It is somewhere east of sunset
> And it's somewhere west of dawn.
>
> So come, you merry voyageurs,
> With your paddles and bateaux,
> To the land of sky-blue waters
> Where the north-bound rivers flow.
> We will search the wide-flung wilderness
> For the lake where peace lives on.
> It is somewhere east of sunset
> And it's somewhere west of dawn.

III

THE DOUBLE CROSS—AND STILL-MO

It is probable that never has another canoe had such tender handling as we gave Buddie in those first hours. We felt guilty if we scraped the hull against a reed, or permitted the shore brush to touch a rail.

When we reached the island we ran aground so gently that there was not a grind or a jolt. Quickly we unloaded ourselves and the few articles we had brought along. Then we lifted the craft and placed it upside down on the rack that had been built for it. The heavier baggage could be brought over in other boats. Buddie's strength must be conserved for special occasions. I suggested that all it needed was a pillow and someone to sing it to sleep, but my attempted witticism did not get a smile out of Giny. Buddie's condition was no laughing matter. In the days to come all the calking, gluing, patching and varnishing possible would be done to that thin, shapely hull.

Now that we had landed at our island, full realization that we were once again in our forest Sanctuary crept over us. We dug up a bit of the sacred soil with our toes, pinched off some balsam needles and held them to our nostrils to get the fragrance, picked up some dry leaves and fondled them, then let our eyes wander from one loved object to another. This was *home*—the most beautiful spot on earth, in our not-too-humble opinion. At once the interval since our departure months ago collapsed to utter nothingness. What space in memory was there for the trials and tribulations of a lecture tour? Had not our hearts been here all the time? We had caught up with them, and now recovered from the illusion that we had ever been away. This moment we could be just returning from a trip to town for supplies. Perhaps we had only taken a turn around the lake shore. At least there was no time but now, no place but here, and in our thoughts that moment it seemed that this was all that had ever been.

We walked slowly to a point where we might pause and look quietly on our inviting little cabin. How could such a volume of comfort, security and happiness come out of a thing so modest and unpretentious? There had been uncounted evenings of good fellowship with friends, days of sunny brilliance, hours upon hours of books and many periods used in quiet thought. There were music and writing, wholesome conversation and homey security.

Giny directed my attention to a neat little hole which had been chewed under the eaves into the cabin attic. Whatever animal had done this was able to enter it from the roof of the kitchen. We always act indignant and complain a lot when such things happen, but since some creature is always chewing holes in our house, there was no need to be particularly concerned about this one. Nor were we left in the dark long as to who had done it. Through the opening came crawling a saucy-looking red squirrel. It jumped to the roof, eyed us and then began chattering excitedly.

"Still-Mo!" Giny called. "It is Still-Mo, look at that tail."

Yes, it was Still-Mo. That bushy tail was an indisputable mark of identification. Through an accident, the

creature had lost half of its tail when quite young. Later the hair of this tail had become very thick and bushy like a feather duster.

"Hi, there, Still-Mo, you rascal!" I called. "Do you know you are written into a book? Not that you care a bit!" Giny carried on the conversation with the creature and it chattered back an endless stream of things we could not begin to understand.

Yes, even at that moment the book *Eeny, Meeny, Miney,*

Mo—and *Still-Mo* was with the publishers. Nature lovers were soon to begin reading about this very chickaree that had chewed a hole in our attic and now stood there looking down at us. Still-Mo held a prominent place in the book. I had given him a great build-up, in line with my most honest convictions. He was the big he-man of the red-squirrel family. His was the kind of character which, in men, makes the explorer, the adventurer, the seeker of remote places, the doer of great and valiant things. When barely six weeks old, Still-Mo had climbed our highest trees and explored the most remote corners of the island. While the rest of his family yet held to baby ways, he was reaching out into the world. We saw him swim to a neighboring island and back again. He swam to the mainland and returned. He was pushing back his horizons, and no deed seemed too difficult or dangerous for him to attempt. Surely this was a super-squirrel among squirrels, the type that in our race gives us our Columbuses, Admiral Byrds, our Livingstones and Stanleys.

As I was pondering this thought, Still-Mo had disappeared through the new attic doorway. An instant later Giny caught my arm. "Look!" she said excitedly. "Sam, we have been double-crossed!"

Still-Mo had reappeared, jumping down to the roof. Immediately another little red head had peaked out of the hole and looked around with an impudent expression. It was the chattering image of Still-Mo. The awful truth dawned on me. Still-Mo was not a great "he-man" at all—Still-Mo was a mother.

"Heavens! *More-Mo?*" I exclaimed, looking at the youngster. More-Mo has been the name of that squirrel ever since.

As More-Mo dropped down and scampered about the roof awkwardly, another little head appeared at the opening!

"Two-Mo! Help!" cried Giny, throwing up her arms—and Two-Mo it was who jumped down and ran up to his unintentionally deceiving mother.

Still a third little head looked out of the hole in our attic!

"No-Mo! Please!" I called, and thus was the third one christened.

Still-Mo seemed very proud of her children More-Mo, Two-Mo and No-Mo. She was quite unapologetic for the mix-up she had made. It seemed to me I saw a grin on her face as she looked down at us with a sly wink—though of course in my bewildered state of mind at that moment I could imagine almost anything. What was I to do? Certainly, I couldn't do anything with Still-Mo, so at first opportunity I wired my publishers. "A terrible inaccuracy in my book," my telegram read. "Still-Mo has double-crossed us and turned out to be a lady. She is nursing triplets in our attic, and doesn't care whether we like it or not. Can you hold up the book until I make some corrections or else drive Still-Mo out of the country so no one will ever see her? As a famous Hollywood star would say, 'I'm mortified! I'm humiliated!'"

The unconsoling reply came, "Sorry, but the book is

already on the press. Too late to do anything but hide your face. Tell Still-Mo for us we'll pay two bushels of acorns of hush money if she will keep quiet about the whole affair."

Even on the morning of our arrival, I knew that Still-Mo and her jabbering youngsters would never keep quiet about anything. They chattered and screamed at one another while they raced in and out of our attic, sometimes jumping about on the thin boards overhead until it sounded as if some horses had gone through that tiny hole.

"Maybe you would like something hot to drink," said Giny with a meaning look. "You are pale and fagged out. Is something bothering you?"

"I could choim like a squoip!" I said, and then made a record hundred-yard dash just ahead of a flying broom.

IV

SIX LITTLE SAUSAGES

GINY and I have become convinced that names are vastly important. We share in the popular fault of forgetting the names of acquaintances and friends, but we know that to remember them would be better manners. You are closer to anything or anyone you can call by name, and a feeling of possession comes with the use of a designating title. It is for this reason that Giny and I name things whether animate or inanimate.

We faced a new problem in dealing out names that first day. When we had recovered somewhat from the shock of Still-Mo's double cross, and had completed the first tasks of moving into our home, we found time to look around. We were immediately impressed with the evidence of fresh digging we saw. Little piles of sand and gravel in a dozen spots marked the entrances to some newly made underground homes. We had no doubt as to what animal had done this. Very soon our convictions were substantiated. Looking out of one of the holes was a tiny animal, brownish gray in color, with ears shaped like little seashells, eyes that stared unblinkingly as if formed of glass, and a homely face now made even less attractive by a coating of sand and dust. As we watched, another of like description peeked out timidly from under a shed.

Still another popped out from a different hole, and a fourth went scooting through the brush. Of a sudden the island seemed to have sprouted baby woodchucks or groundhogs. They were appearing from every side, looking at us with infantile curiosity and dashing hither and yon with apparently no object other than to be on the move. Though the first impression was that there were at least two dozen, when we got to the bottom of the matter we learned that there were only six of them.

Of course, the little fellows were quite welcome. Our island is not large enough to support so many woodchucks, but we could bring in food for them until nature distributed them about the country-side. But they must be named—that was the real problem. Six good names are not easy to think up in a hurry.

We had some idea of what they should be called, however. Our readers will remember earlier books in which was told the story of our original woodchuck pet named Sausage because she was ground hog. It was her pun name. One of Sausage's offspring, named Link Sausage, had established her residence on the Isle of Patmos. The sextuplets we looked upon now were her young—that is, little Sausages. Therefore we named one chubby chuck *Thuringer*—a name that eventually was reduced to "Yethir." A second one was distinguished by his actions. Obviously he was an irritable youngster, snarling and biting at his family. He bit everyone, bit his brothers, bit his sisters, even bit his own mother. He was the worst brat of the group, so we named him *Bratwurst*. A third one was a jitterbug! She was dancing around all the time, never still for a moment, so we called her *Salami*. Number four was a retiring, quiet little creature whom we named *Wiener*. Number five was christened *Patty*. Patty Sausage later proved to be our favorite. Perhaps it was because he drew sympathy. He was the runt of the family and sort of a natural punching bag. All the others were larger and stronger than he, and he was constantly being bossed, abused and pushed around. He had the faculty of being in the wrong place at the right time. Whenever either of us stepped on or kicked a creature unintentionally, it was sure to be Patty. When we dropped something, it generally lighted on Patty.

Then came the naming of number six. He was easy to identify both by his manner and by his appearance. In size he exceeded the others considerably. He was a born prankster, a practical joker, and in every action just a smart alec. I have seen him make a run at little Patty, strike him unexpectedly from behind and send him rolling and squealing down a hillside. Others must stay back from food until he had his fill, even though there would be enough for an army of woodchucks. He bullied the entire family. As days went on, he picked on us too. He chewed up the door mat, left teeth marks on doors and sills, chewed up a towel and ate a cake of soap I left within his reach, and bit holes in my best breeches. At first we just referred to him as *Smart Alec* or *Old Number Six*. But one day when I watched him going around looking for trouble and finding it, I waved my hand in disgust and exclaimed, "Oh, Bologna!" *O. Bologna* has been his name ever since!

Link Sausage and her tribe—Thuringer, Bratwurst, Salami, Wiener, Patty and O. Bologna—certainly honeycombed our island with their network of underground homes. O. Bologna dug one tunnel right under the cornerstone of our cabin. He would! We located eighteen entrances to their caves. Probably there were others in the brush that we did not find.

However, we loved our little family of ground hogs. There is no creature in the forest more awkward and homely, and from the human viewpoint, there are few creatures of less value than the woodchuck. His hide isn't worth the taking, he isn't very good as food, he eats much and plants nothing. There is little to love him for except his pudgy little self. And maybe right there we see a virtue. It is good to love for no reason. Love that is bestowed in compensation for some favor or blessing has selfishness mixed in. We had to love the six Sausages just because they were alive. They couldn't do anything for us except give us a chance to love them. And after all, I believe that is enough.

V

A CANOE AND A QUANDARY

WE USED Buddie, the canoe, frequently those June days and evenings. The old craft creaked and groaned when we lifted it; it shed slivers as a porky does its quills; it let in little samples of lake water occasionally—but it stayed afloat and held its proud head up as jauntily as ever. The worst leaks were stopped temporarily and the weakest places strengthened by one means or another. Pieces of canvas were fastened here and there, glue poured into cracks and varnish added layer upon layer until Giny said she felt as if she were sailing around in just a coat of paint. Buddie's efficiency was not impaired in the least, however. It responded to the paddle as well as in its best days. And at night, when we couldn't see the patches, it looked as beautiful as ever.

Fortunately, June offered us many quiet evenings. Waters were habitually calm and glasslike. For a few nights the moon looked down upon the forest world through a thin veil of springtime moisture. The soft light gave fairylike beauty to solitude. Buddie fitted perfectly into the picture. The broad beam kept it from sinking deeply, and sometimes it seemed not to dent the water on which it rested.

We renewed our acquaintance with old haunts. Up

the creek we found beavers were building a new house and starting a new dam. Along the north shore, where an ancient animal runway comes down to the water's edge, we saw deer occasionally. However, we could not expect them to be numerous at this season. This was fawning time. Back in the secret chambers of the forest, little spotted, wide-eyed Bambis were staring up at the great, bewildering woodland world into which they had been born. Does were busy with the care of their little ones.

We discovered that bears were around. They were seldom seen, but we found their tracks and heard their grunts. We saw one of our old raccoons, but these animals also were busy with family problems. Once in the gray light of dusk the fluid form of a woods coyote soundlessly emerged from a balsam thicket, crossed a little clearing, and disappeared into the dark depths of a hemlock grove. The Sanctuary was teeming with life.

One of these first days was made brighter by a letter from Sandy the Squoip. He said he had been half ashamed to write the letter. Apparently there had been other mail started to us, but lost or delayed somewhere in war-zone confusion. He had written us before that he came through the fighting without a scratch. Hadn't even taken the crease out of his breeches, he said. Then—the disgrace of it!—he had gone to England and there was struck by one of our own jeeps. Lots of Packards around, and he had to be hit by a jeep! For no reason at all, as he expressed it, he was put in a hospital. He insisted it was just curiosity. The doctors wanted to know why a jeep couldn't make a dent in him. "I should have been home long before this," he wrote. "We rate a rest furlough and then we will head for that other war we've been hearing about. I'll be coming your way, and I can't decide which I want to see most—you or Buddie."

"Now what are we going to do?" Giny asked with concern. "Buddie is having all it can do to hold together from day to day."

"I'll have a talk with that canoe," I said with a one-sided smile. "Buddie will hold together for Sandy. But just to make sure, I am going to town."

"What for?"

"Buckets of glue, gallons of varnish, yards of canvas and plenty of wire, string and some adhesive tape!"

"Maybe a little chewing gum would help, too," suggested Giny.

VI

A LISP ALONG A FOREST TRAIL

It is a mighty good plan to enjoy getting fire wood if you are going to live in the north country. Getting wood is something that must be done, particularly if you have a fireplace. A fireplace is the supreme part of a home, and I wouldn't want to be without one. But it has an appetite that knows no end. No snowdrift could melt faster than a woodpile does in the late fall and early spring days. However much is put up in reserve, the hour will come sure as taxes and faster when you have to go "a-wood-gettin'." Yes, it is much better to like it, because you have to do it anyway.

There is never a spring or an autumn when our woodpile does not get close to the vanishing point. The spring in which this story began was no exception. The once-impressive mound of sixteen-inch hardwood chunks had reached the place where I was scratching about in the leaves to find the few pieces that might have hidden there. It was high time for "wood-gettin'."

On a warm, clear morning when there was just a touch of that old human laziness commonly called spring fever in the air, I loaded my sawbuck, crosscut saw and ax in the boat and rowed to the mainland. Birds were mighty happy. For a few moments I wished I was built like them, with a coat of feathers to keep me warm so that I wouldn't have to go sawing wood, and could just sit on a limb of a tree and sing. But by the time I had located and lifted the first two logs I was warmed to my job and grateful that I could saw and chop. I found dry cedar for kindling and near at hand a tall, perfectly seasoned yellow birch just yearning for the fireplace. Cutting was done as close to the water as possible so that the wood could be taken to the island conveniently.

I was working near our old Friendship Trail that wandered through the forest to cabins of friends on the shore of a neighboring lake. Salt, a pet porcupine now several years old, appeared in one of the trees I inspected. I knew him instantly. He came down the tree hurriedly, tail first as usual, and stopped about four feet from the ground, hanging to the bark and looking at me.

"Salt, you prickly old rascal!" I cried as I went up to him. "Where have you been, and where is your pal Pepper?" The story of Salt and Pepper has been told before, but there are always new pages to add to their book. Salt eyed me for a moment, and then started playing in his characteristic way. I had hoped to see him during our summer hikes, but I feared lest he had outgrown his play. Not in the least. He dodged back and forth on the tree trunk, looking at me from one side and then the other. He got to the ground and chased me around, causing me to use both time and energy that had been promised to the woodpile. Presently he stopped, sat up, snorted, made some abrupt decision and went hustling away into the forest, possibly for some forgotten appointment.

I went back to the neglected task of the day, all smiles and chuckles at having found this little forest friend. There is some special kind of pleasure in meeting a forest creature who has been a pet, and who still remembers us. Giny and I never cease to thrill at such an adventure. It would be so easy for them to forget us in the long months while we are away. Living is difficult for them and problems many. Therefore it impresses us as being a triumph of friendship when they hold memory of us and show pleasure at our infrequent meetings.

Other familiar creatures came to me that day. There was Stubby, the chipmunk now in his fourth year, who raced up unhesitatingly, ran out on the log I was sawing and jumped to my shoulder. I had come prepared for his visit, and dealt out some peanuts with which my pockets bulged. A few moments later came Nuisance, the old red squirrel, now in his sixth year. Gray hairs were mixed with the red, but he was as active as ever. A peanut tossed within his reach sent him away rejoicing. And, of course, wood-getting was not receiving all the attention promised it.

There was a fine maple log on the sawbuck and the saw was singing its way through it, when off in the forest I heard a human voice. I listened intently. The tones were those of a child in considerable excitement, though at first I could not make out what was being said. Obviously the owner of the voice was coming down Friendship Trail, and since there was no cry of alarm or distress, I waited. Words were becoming more distinct, though they had a peculiar flourish to them that kept me guessing.

"*P*ea**nut-th!** *P*ea**nut-th!**" lisped the oncomer. "Here I come, an' I got *p*ea**nut-th!**"

The words had a hop and a skip to them, as though some youngster were dancing through the forest in the style of Peter Pan.

"Th-tubby! Noothanth! I got *p*eanut-th," the happy voice went on. "Come an' get 'em. *P*ea**nut-th,** *p*ea**nut-th!**"

The sound and the soundmaker drew nearer. When he came to view he was just what I had expected—a round-faced, rosy-cheeked, chubby boy of about nine. He was merrily skipping along carrying a brown paper bag in one hand.

I felt inclined to envy the little fellow his innocent

freedom. His was an enchanted world, I could tell by the way he looked eagerly from side to side. Maybe there was just a little tinge of fear present in him, not of being harmed, but that the very things he imagined were there might actually be. For he was at that sublime state of growth where fairies could be flittering about in the luxuriant foliage overhead. Brownies could be scurrying among the leaves. Gnomes could be peering out at him from shadows. Indian braves, chieftains and princesses, overlooked by the white man's sweeping advance, could be encamped just over the top of the nearest knoll. And right around any bend in the trail he might enter a realm of magic where trees could speak to him, animals call him by name and all the marvels of Alice-in-Wonderland be spread before him.

"*Pea*nut-th! *Pea*nut-t-th! Th-tubby, Noothanth—I got peanut-t-th." The youngster was nearing the spot where I stood, still unnoticed. I suppose he suffered a bit of a shock when I brought him to an abrupt halt.

"Hello there!" I called.

His feet stirred up the leaves of the trail as he applied the brakes. He looked up. Had one of those trees spoken to him?

"How are you, young feller?" I went on, his eyes now finding me.

"Oh-h-h-h!" he said, probably both relieved and disappointed to find that this greeting came from anything so prosaic as a human being. Then he took a second look, his eyes grew wide with excitement, and his mouth opened a little. I wondered if there was a fairy standing behind me to cause all this emotion.

"You're—you're—Tham Cammel, huh?" He could hardly get the words out.

"Why, yes, I am Sam Campbell," I said, wondering whether in view of his wild-eyed attitude I ought to be proud or ashamed of the fact.

"Yes—you're Tham Cammel."

I was glad he agreed. "But who are you?" I asked, walking forward and extending my hand. He laid his hand in mine, thumb and all, co-operated with me in just one shake, and then drew away.

"Don't you know my name?" he asked, looking a little disappointed.

I was embarrassed. "No, it doesn't come to my mind right off. You know," I assumed a confidential tone, "I have a terrible time remembering names. Sometimes I forget my own."

"Your name is Tham Cammel," he volunteered.

"Yes, I know. But I can't recall yours. Now where did we know each other."

"At my th-chool!" he said, with a disarming smile.

"Yes, but what school is that?"

"Don't you know my th-chool's name either?" He was quite disgusted by this time.

"Well, you see I go to lots of schools," I said lamely. "I think I remember though. I showed pictures at your school, didn't I?"

Of course I had shown pictures at hundreds of schools

during recent months, so this was a fairly safe assumption. However, the words delighted him. He laughed in a funny little way that I learned later was quite characteristic. It began with a *whe-e-e* and ended with a *hick,* and denoted something had happened that was extremely pleasing.

"Now you know, I gueth, huh?" He was pleased.

"Yes, but I haven't thought of the name of the school as yet. Just what was it?" I furroughed my eyebrows.

My little lad had become suddenly preoccupied. His eyes sparkled under the glow of some exciting internal vision. A laugh started deep down inside and then broke out almost violently. "Ho, ho, ho!" He pointed his finger at me accusingly. "Oh, Th-tinkey! Th-tinkey!"

This could have been mistaken for discourtesy, but it was not so intended. He wasn't calling me "Stinkey." Rather were his words and his laugh rising from a recollection in which I was beginning to share. It was of a huge auditorium in an old school, located in a poor and crowded district of a Midwestern city. I had come there to show motion pictures of our Sanctuary animals. As I stood on the platform making some introductory remarks, the audience of youngsters burst out in loud laughter. I hadn't said anything funny and I looked around to see if I were sharing the stage with other performers. I was! Out from the wings came three boys of about the ten year notch—and trotting along with them, led by a leash, was a real live skunk!

The joke had long been planned. During a number of

such visits I had been telling these children of my forest friends. Now they had one to show me. While the audience continued to reel with laughter, I met "Stinkey" face to face. The little animal was the loved pet of the boy who led him. Stinkey had been deodorized, properly bathed and perfumed for this occasion, and I found him a most appealing creature.

It took many minutes for the pupils to calm down so that my lecture could continue.

I remembered the name of the school now. How could one ever forget it after such an experience? It is just as well to withhold it here lest the incident related above embarrass the faculty. But I said the name correctly to the boy in the forest that day, much to his delight.

"Yeth!" he said, giving his funny little laugh. "Now, what-th my name?"

He looked all ready to be disappointed if I failed. There were eleven hundred students in the auditorium that time, and I was supposed to know his name!

Now I was finding something familiar about his little face. The experience at the school was becoming clearer. After the program a number of autograph seekers had come to me. Yes, one *was* a talkative little fellow who lisped! His all-too-fertile imagination had been stirred by what he saw, by thoughts of the great forest and the animals.

"I wuth in a jungle wunth," he had shouted at me over the din of those requesting autographs.

"Were you?" I had found a chance to say. "Where was it?"

"Oh, a long long way off," he said with a gesture indicating it was much too far for me to comprehend.

"How far?" I called, now determined to know of this remote country.

"'Way, 'way off," he said, pointing more up than in any particular direction, and then he added a description calculated to floor me. "It wuth ten mileth from Chicago."

"Amazing!" I commented. "What did you see there?"

"Oh, I heard a big noith one night," he began, his eyes widening. "I heard a big noith one night——" He stopped; the old imagination just wasn't functioning fast enough.

"Did you go out to see what it was?" I asked, determined that I wasn't going to be cheated out of this story. One can never tell what will happen ten miles from Chicago!

"Oh, yeth," he said, relieved to have thought of something. "I went out, and what do you think it wuth?"

"I don't know, what wuth it?" My own tongue was getting tangled.

"You gueth."

"I don't want to guess, you tell me."

"Well." He drew in a deep breath as if it were going to take a lot of power even to speak of this fearful experience. "Well—there wuth a wildcat!"

Amazing! Inconceivable! "What was the wildcat doing?" I asked.

The little fellow's eyes were almost popping out by this time, and he was flushed with excitement. "There wuth that wildcat, and he wuth, he wuth——" The story wasn't coming out so well, but suddenly he caught the theme. "He wuth scrachin' my eyeth out!" he declared as he looked around to see how many would faint at this account of jungle savagery.

"That is a mighty wonderful experience," I was saying to him, as the teachers turned their heads away to hide their snickers. "I'm glad you told me." The youngster was all wound up now, and I am sure there was another terrific adventure about to be related—maybe even farther from Chicago. But I headed him off.

"What is your name," I asked.

"Huh?"

"What is your name?"

"Oh—Daddy call-th me 'Bub.'"

"But you have another name, what else does he call you?"

"Oh—he call-th me 'Hi-Bub.'"

That was all I got. The situation was relieved as a teacher took him by the hand and led him away. I called after him, "Good-by, Hi-Bub," and "Good-by, Tham Cammel," he called back. I had not seen him since, but there was no doubt of it. This was Hi-Bub standing before me on the trail at my Sanctuary!

"Ho! Ho!" I put my arm about his shoulder. "I knew you all the time—Hi-Bub!"

He gave his laugh, starting with a *whee-e-e* and ending with a *hick*.

It was fine to be remembered.

"But how did you come here?" I asked. "The nearest cabin down that trail is about a mile away. Where did you come from?"

After a lot of lisping, questions and counter-questions, I got his story. His mother and daddy had heard little else from him except northwoods—morning, noon and night. He wanted to go there. He wanted to see "Tham Cammel." Then there was something which his little talk did not make clear to me. But I gathered his daddy had to go where there were "thunshine and quiet." So it seemed that partly because of Hi-Bub's persistent enthusiasm and partly because of his daddy, they came north. They had found a cabin for rent at the far end of Friendship Trail. Someone had told them that the trail led to our Sanctuary. So—Bub had followed it.

"Then you weren't afraid to go through the woods alone, were you, Hi-Bub?" I commented.

"No, you thaid nothing in the woodth would hurt me," he answered.

Yes, I had said that—and I was glad to find it had made such an impression.

"Well, nothing will hurt you," I agreed. "And you knew too that you wouldn't get lost?"

"Yeth, you thaid to thtay on a trail and we wouldn't get lotht."

I had said that too, though I didn't know that one of those little fellows was going to put my advice to a test so soon.

"Well, all right, Bub, you made it. When you go home I want to walk with you and see that you do follow the trail properly. Now what do you want to do?"

"I got peanut-th." Bub waved the paper bag. "And I want to feed Th-tubby and Noothanth. What-th that?"

He pointed excitedly toward one of the logs I had been sawing.

"Why, that is Stubby now," I said. "You may feed him if——" But Bub was way ahead of me. He had taken a peanut from the bag, and before I could stop him he ran toward Stubby yelling, "Look, Th-tubby, I got peanut-th. Come on, Th-tubby!" Stubby didn't come on. In fact, his reaction was quite the reverse. Bub's enthusiastic approach frightened the creature until in its hurried flight it almost left its striped hide behind. Bub met with calamity too. He stubbed his toe and fell flat, his bag opening and scattering peanuts far and wide.

There were no tears. Bub was too much of a man for that. We gathered up the peanuts, after which I gave him some lessons in approaching animals. It took some time to convince "Noothanth" and "Th-tubby" that all was well. The sun was low in the west before he finally had the thrill of these simple creatures coming up to him and climbing all over him, while he dispensed his supply of peanuts.

Then we went down the trail through the forest to his cabin together. I asked him to lead the way so that I could test his skill. He proved himself perfectly capable of trail travel. When I met his parents I found them concerned and about to start in search of him. They had thought the distance down the trail to be less than it was. I assured them that Bub was welcome to come back when he wished, but I recommended that they walk with him over the trail several times to make sure he became accustomed to it. This they did later. It was a good wide trail, well marked, and nothing could harm him if he held to it.

As I started away and they were entering the cabin, I heard the mother speak to Bub.

"What did you see in the woods?" she asked.

"Well, Th-tubby and Noothanth were there."

"What else?"

"Oh-h-h, there wuth a great big wildcat and-d-d-d——"

The door closed behind them, and I never learned if Bub's eyes were scratched out again or not.

VII

SUPER-SENSE AND NON-SENSE

WOOD-GETTING was much improved the next day after my initial visit with Hi-Bub. I attribute my success mainly to the fact he didn't show up. By quitting time, little piles of freshly split logs were in evidence along the shore line, marking spots where the right kind of trees had been found and given the saw and ax treatment. It was with a feeling of triumph that I brought the first boatload back that evening, and proudly offered Giny a gratefire made of personally selected, well-seasoned, hand-prepared wood.

After dinner we took a short paddle about the lake, just "to give Buddie some exercise," as Giny said. A spell of springtime cold had crept in, and the forest was drawing shawls of fog about its shoulders. The landscape presented some fantastic effects. Over banks of mist, treetops appeared, seeming to be detached from the earth. Stars found little windows in the earth cloud through which to peek and coyly wink. Buddie seemed almost self-propelled in this mystic world. We had to give but light strokes with our paddles, and the canoe glided on endlessly. While in a thicket of fog there was no feeling of motion, yet suddenly we would emerge to find ourselves drifting along in velvety smoothness, the water not even ruffled at our passing.

Loons must call on a night like that. Two of them did. At first they were far separated, obviously resting on the surface of the water. Then came a call from one side of the lake, to be answered from the opposite shore. Unquestionably they were having fun, for there was actual joy in their voices. One of them confirmed a conviction I have long held, that loons play with echoes. This old fellow would give a brief, sharp cry. It went reverberating down the opposite shore line. He was perfectly still—listening. His mate co-operated by keeping silent, too. When the last echo had sounded—and not until then—the creature called again. Once more he listened entranced, while the shores bounced his cry back and forth like a ping-pong ball. He did this at least a dozen times. Then, tired of this little game, the two birds broke out into that wild shrieking that sounds like a Zulu looks. They took to wing, piercing the fog banks, once passing so low over our heads we could hear the soft whistle of their wings.

We now returned to our island, which was just a little bundle of black forest, floating in an infinitude of mist and mystery. At the cabin we selected two books, moved favorite chairs before the fireplace, and prepared for an evening of hut happiness. I kindled the fire with shreds of birchbark and slivers cut from a dry cedar log. The flames grew, fed by moderate sticks of pine from the hill at Point Trail's End, and gained body and permanence with sizable logs of hemlock and birch found along Friendship Trail. With both cedar and hemlock in there—

old gossips that they are—it was a talkative fire. It popped and crackled and hissed and sometimes lisped like Hi-Bub.

My book lay open and so far unread in my lap, while I practiced at Bub's fine art of imagining. It seemed to me the fire was reminiscing, and I was trying to gain from its babble the story of what the trees whose wood now burned had seen through the years as they stood stanchly among the legions of the forest. I glanced over at Giny. Her book also rested in her lap, opened and unread. Maybe that is why books are such good friends. They are not easily offended.

I noticed that Giny's eyes were dwelling on a toy birch-bark canoe that lay on the fireplace mantel. The tiny craft had been modeled after the design of our beloved Buddie. Little smiles of pleasure played about her lips, and I saw she was living through some happy thoughts. I gazed at the toy for a few moments and soon I was having dreams too.

"Giny," I said, breaking the silence.

She looked up startled, as if surprised to find that there was anyone else in the world. "Yes?"

"I am discovering amazing powers within myself," I began, assuming an attitude of extreme importance.

"What now?" She never knew what to expect.

"Well—I am a mind reader—probably the greatest in the world!"

She looked at me in a way that made me back up a little.

"Well, I'll say the greatest in America."

A crooked smile deflated me still more.

"Now I am sure I am the greatest mind reader in Wisconsin!"

"That still is a lot of territory," she insisted.

"Well, I am the most remarkable mind reader in this cabin—" and by way of being perfectly safe I added, "—on this side of the room."

Her smile indicated there was no further argument. "What is all this about?" she asked.

"Simply this. I know just what you are thinking right now, and I can prove it."

She awaited the proof.

"You were thinking of Buddie!" I said.

She nodded and smiled. I closed my eyes and clustered the fingers of one hand against my forehead as if I were entering some sort of trance.

"You were thinking of a young man too—tall, handsome, with light curly hair. You call him Sandy—but wait, there is more to his name. It is a funny name. Now I get it. His name is Sandy the Squoip!"

Giny laughed. "Simply amazing!" she said. "Please go on."

I was becoming enthusiastic now. "And you were thinking of a lake. Let's see, now, it is a strange kind of lake. You have never seen it. You don't know where it is. Yet you dwell in fancy among its charms and beauties. You picture animals there, and wilderness and solitude. Why, you have even named this fancied place! It is Sanctuary Lake!"

"I am simply dumfounded!" said Giny. "Where have you been hiding this remarkable gift all these years? What else was I thinking?"

I had to pause a moment to get deeper in my "trance," and besides I had to fish around for ideas.

"This man Sandy the Squoip you expect to come here soon. Once you promised him that we would go with him and Buddie in search of Sanctuary Lake. Now you wonder if it could be done while he is here this coming visit. You wonder if Buddie would be equal to such a thing. You don't how it would be possible to make such a trip, but you wish it could be done. You don't even know where we would get the gas to run our car up into the far north. You believe we would have no right to put that wear on our tires. You know the ration board doesn't approve of using cars merely for pleasure."

"And now," Giny broke into my trance sharply, "I am a mind reader. You have been thinking those same things, and you aren't reading my mind, you are exposing your own thoughts. You want to go searching for Sanctuary Lake when Squoip gets here."

Then she asked the question that took the life out of our little illusion.

"Is there—is there any way it could be done?"

I put some more wood on the fire and became more practical. "I can't see how it could be possible," I said, disliking my own words.

We picked up and read our friendly, patient books.

VIII

A PORKY PROBLEM AND HI-BUB

THERE were handicaps aplenty in my wood-cutting the next day. I was working hard at extricating a fine-looking log from a tangled pile of brush, when Salt and Pepper, the porcupines, showed up. Pepper, always the shy one, scouted around the wood and the sawbuck for a few minutes, then disappeared into the forest. Not so with Salt. He had the reputation of being a pest, and he made sure I didn't forget it. Suddenly he developed a passionate love for that sawbuck. It was the most important spot in the world to him that moment. I couldn't begin to use the saw without the risk of taking a leg off of him. When I carried him away, he squealed resentfully—and got back faster than I did. Once he strayed off a few feet to sniff around the pieces of newly cut wood. I thought maybe he was through bothering me, so I went into the brush and got a section of log that was about all I could lift. I came back with it on my shoulder, my muscles aching under the load, and walked up wanting to deposit the log in position for sawing. Salt made a dash for the sawbuck and climbed up on it. Steadying the log on my overburdened shoulder with one hand, I picked him up with the other and put him on the ground. I tried to put the log in place before he could climb back, but it was too heavy to move quickly. Salt got right where the log ought to be. I pleaded with him, I coaxed, I threatened, but he stayed on, grunting softly about how contented he was. Then I conceived a plan that worked. Using my last bit of strength I reached down with one hand, picked him up, and swung him on top of the log that was now burrowing right into my shoulder. Then I put the whole burden, Salt and the log, on the sawbuck—and sat down to recover from my exertion, if possible.

Salt finally tired of his pestering, though not nearly so soon as I had. However, he could do something about it, whereas I couldn't. He sauntered off to a tree, climbed to a comfortable crotch and went fast asleep.

I actually tiptoed around. The last thing in the world I wanted to do right then was awaken that porcupine. If he should outdo Rip Van Winkle's record, it would be all right with me.

For a few minutes I had a chance to work, but the opportunity didn't last long. Far back in the forest I heard a voice calling. I couldn't make out a word, and yet I knew full well what was being said.

"Peanut-th! Peanut-th! Th-tubby and Noothanth—I got peanut-th!"

Hi-Bub was coming! I sawed at double time and swung the ax until I looked something like a windmill, but I couldn't get much done before he arrived. When he was approaching I went to meet him a little way down the trail, to ask his co-operation.

A PORKY PROBLEM AND HI-BUB

"Hi-Bub!" I said.

"Hello, Tham Cammel!" he answered, with his own original little laugh. "I got peanut-th."

"I see you have. Stubby and Nuisance will be glad to get them. Did you have any trouble following the trail?"

"Nope!" said Bub, with a shake of the head, "exthept I thaw a bear."

It could be—and on the other hand this might be the beginning of another jungle tale.

"A big bear?" I asked, and it was the wrong question.

"Oh-o-o!" said Bub, looking around for something to compare it to. "It wath bigger'n a cow!" His excitement grew. "It wuth a mama bear and th-he had thix cub-th!"

"Why didn't you make it five, Bub? It would be easier for you to say."

"Five, then," said Bub. Anything to be obliging!

A marvelous story unfolded, punctuated by laughs and lisps. It seems that these bear cubs had been bad, so the mother bear picked them up one at a time and administered a spanking. Hi-Bub had stood there and watched it all. How grand it is to be an eyewitness to such things, for there is just no question of the authenticity of such an experience when you have seen it with your own eyes, the way Hi-Bub had. I said as much to him, but wished I hadn't for he started in to say "authenticity" and I was afraid he wouldn't last through it.

"But the bears didn't frighten you and they didn't hurt you, did they, Bub?" I said, hoping to bring the story to an end with the moral that animals won't harm you if you don't harm them.

Bub headed off the point. "Yeth!" he declared, his face taking on that wildcat-scratching-my-eye-out look.

"Did they eat you up, Bub?" I asked anxiously.

"No!" And then incredulously, "Don't you thee me here?"

"Oh, I'm sorry. How did you escape?"

It took a minute to figure this out, but he found an answer. Believe it or not, Inky, my old porcupine, whom Hi-Bub had seen in pictures and of whom he had read in a book, showed up that very moment and chased the bears away! Most extraordinary, I know—but then Inky is a very unusual porcupine.

"Inky wath thwell," went on Bub, enthusiastically. "He thtayed with me, walked all the way—I gueth to thee I didn't get lotht."

"I suppose he carried your bag of peanuts for you, didn't he?" I suggested, hoping to make some contribution to this adventure.

Hi-Bub looked at me reproachfully. "Huh-uh. I gueth you jutht made that up!"

I gave up!

Under request for the utmost silence, I led Hi-Bub over to the tree where Salt was snoozing, and pointed out the homely little bundle of quills and hair.

"What—?" asked Bub.

"It is Salt, the porcupine, Bub. You know, like Inky that you—er—met on the trail today."

Bub stared long and curiously, suggesting the idea that he had never seen a porcupine before.

"Will he come down?" he asked.

"Yes, but we don't want him now. He gets in my way when I am working. I want you to be as quiet as you can, so you don't awaken him. Now suppose you go down the trail a way and call Stubby and Nuisance. Don't call loud so you wake up Salt, just quiet-like."

The appeal seemed to be effective at first. Bub looked at Salt for a few minutes, then carefully picked his steps and made off a little way down the trail. I heard him call in subdued tones for the chipmunk and squirrel, and knew by his words of greeting that they had responded. I had got fairly into the wood-cutting when suddenly I discovered Bub back again, right under Salt's bedroom tree.

"Ith he awake yet?" he said in a whisper that was a little louder than a shout.

"No. Sh-h-h-h! Don't stir him up, he'll bother the life out of me."

Bub looked up at the slumbering porcupine, and suddenly developed a political cough.

"A-hem!" he went, vehemently, looking up to see if the sound had any effect.

"A-hem! a-hem!" he continued, with such vigor that a real cough resulted. Still Salt slept on. Then Bub started to sing. It was the "Star Spangled Banner," so I couldn't ask him to stop. Patriotically, I stopped my work and stood at attention. This was a losing battle for me anyway. Surely Bub's solo was far from a slumber song. About the place where he began to ask if the "Thtar Thpangled Ba-an-er-er thtill waveth," Salt was moving about. The porky looked down drowsily at the soloist.

"Oh-h-h! Heth awake!" Bub discovered innocently. If Salt hadn't awakened after what went on, I would have been puzzled as to his real condition.

Salt came slowly down the tree, Bub backing away, not sure whether or not he was glad the nap was over.

"He won't hurt you, Bub," I assured him. "He's just like Inky, and Inky didn't hurt you."

Bub gave me a quick glance and then looked back at the oncoming Salt. He wasn't so certain about these real animals. "Maginary" ones were better in some ways. He could make them do as he wished. And even if one did start to harm him, all he had to do was imagine something to make him stop, such as having a porcupine come up at the right moment to chase a bear away.

"Give him a peanut, Bub," I said. "Salt loves peanuts, only you have to shell them for him."

Bub timidly prepared a peanut and offered it, though the boy looked as if he were all ready for a hundred-yard dash. Salt took the food in his usual docile way. A second peanut erased more of the fear in each of them. A third one furthered the job. By the time a dozen had been fed, Salt the porcupine was standing right at the boy's feet reaching up anxiously for more donations, and Bub was laughing delightedly. It was the beginning of a beautiful friendship.

"He'th thwell!" commented my young friend. And apparently Salt reciprocated this newborn devotion.

I tried to renew my work, but without the least hope of success. Bub told me that his parents had instructed him to help "Tham Cammel" cut wood. Why do parents do such things? Between Bub and Salt I couldn't go anywhere or do anything without getting stuck on a porcupine quill or bumping into a boy. Bub's help consisted principally of feeding Salt, though Stubby and Nuisance came in for a little attention. The discouraging angle from my viewpoint was that all of them, Bub included, liked to be right on the sawbuck. I didn't dare use the ax, for whenever I raised it to strike, right where I wanted to hit would appear a chipmunk, a squirrel, a porcupine or a boy. During Hi-Bub's whole afternoon of "helping me" he carried just one piece of wood down to the boat—and he dropped that on my toe!

I started Bub home early by saying that Inky would be waiting for him. He went away assuring me that he would come back tomorrow. Even if he didn't I wasn't to worry, because he'd be sure to come the next day.

"I want to meet Hi-Bub," said Giny as we sat at dinner and I gave her a report of the day's adventure. "You are having all the fun."

"I predict you will have plenty of opportunity," I assured her, with a look that told my feelings more than did my words.

We are bluffers though, we adults. We pretend we are pestered, bothered beyond measure, tried to the limit of endurance by the little ones who in their innocence boss us so easily. But woe be to anyone who would deprive us of our blessed nuisance! It is our privilege to be annoyed and to love it. Our grumblings are a part of our joy. In our hearts is the truth Longfellow put in words:

> Ah! what would the world be to us,
> If the children were no more?
> We should dread the desert behind us
> More than the dark before.

IX

RACKET FROM SOLITUDE

JUNE days floated by like lovely leaflets on the stream of time. July was in the making. The north country was vibrant with humming, buzzing, singing life.

At the Sanctuary, we had got in our wood in spite of all the obstacles Hi-Bub, Salt, Pepper, Stubby, Nuisance, mosquitoes and the weather could provide.

Many of the strange impulses of forest creatures were showing up in the little animals living on our island. The urge to branch out and establish an individual niche in the world had seized our young red squirrels on the island. Once the advice given our youth was "Go west, young man, go west." Nature simply says *go*—go east, west, north, or south—but go! Nature abhors the congregating of her creatures. She fights against the evils of overpopulation. In the hearts of her children she plants an irresistible instinct for spreading, searching out new lands, seeking, ever seeking what lies just beyond the horizon.

Sometimes this urge to go plays strange **little tricks** among the wild folk. They are known to leave a land of plenty and dwell where living is not so good. Yet, this is the lesser of two evils. Nothing else matches the adverse effects of too many dwelling in one area. Better a sparse diet where there is living room. Hence distance is rendered magnetic to the young wild heart. There are, of course, many influences at work in the minds of animals of which we know nothing. They go forth seeking new lands and new homes with such decision and purpose that it seems as if they knew before they started just the log, the tree, the hole in the ground, the cave or the nesting spot in which each would settle.

However, there is something intensely human in the hankering they have for "the old home town." Frequently we see them return, in a visiting sort of way, to the "scenes of their childhood." Witness the actions of Salt and Pepper, or old Inky, the porcupines. Their visits have become less and less frequent, yet for a good portion of their lives they have remembered our Sanctuary and returned periodically. So it was with Rack and Ruin, the raccoons we raised a few years previously. They still return to us, bringing with them generation after generation of offspring. This has been a common experience with all our animal friends.

Still-Mo, the double-crossing red squirrel, moved out of our attic and established herself in a hollow cedar tree near the boathouse. Probably her change of address was upon the insistence of her thoroughly impudent and disrespectful offspring More-Mo. This pugnacious little scamp took a fancy to our attic, and large as it was he had no notion of sharing it. He jabbered and chattered, scolded and chased the other members of his family until they gave up their interest in the old homestead and moved elsewhere. Two-Mo moved down to the point near our island campfire site, and took up abode in an old oak tree which has served as a housing project for many squirrels during the years. No-Mo left the island. I discovered him on the mainland one day while I was sawing wood. He was having quite a run-in with Nuisance. Then for a long time we saw nothing of him.

There were newcomers on our island. We had bats—not in our belfry, but in our boathouse. The odd creatures had found a place where the roofing paper was raised ever so little, yet enough to give them a home. They can fit and be happy in the tiniest places. We watched them often in early evenings as they executed their miraculous flights while gathering in great quantities of mosquitoes and gnats. People do not like bats very well, and for that reason I have been advised not to write about them. But I find our human likes and dislikes are so often founded on fallacies, superstitions and ignorance that I have a tendency always to defend a condemned creature. Our failure to understand the true nature of things has put so many creatures on the undesirable list that if all were destroyed of which people do not approve, there would be little wild life left. There are few living things whose purpose in the great scheme cannot be clearly seen if we get rid of our fears and think wisely.

Bats do not get in your hair, as the popular notion goes. It is the last place in the world they would want to get, and they are adept at missing such entanglement. The bat has a little radar system all his own. Experiments indicate that such remarkable equipment keeps him from bumping into all the things he could easily hit in his night flying. He is not blind, as some people think. His eyes are small, and apparently he depends on them very little, but he has some. His so-called radar equipment makes use of sound waves. He emits high-pitched squeaks as he flies along so erratically. These faint sounds echo back to him from anything in his path, whether it be a thread or a barn, and he changes his course instantly to miss the object.

No doubt this sensitive hearing ability enables him to hear the hum of insects, and directs him in capturing them. His appetite for mosquitoes is so tremendous that a colony of bats will make a noticeable difference in the numbers of these insect pests. One American city is said to have rid itself largely of mosquitoes by introducing an abundance of bats into the region. Yet, it is well not to encourage bats to settle about a dwelling. We do not want them in our house. They do introduce bugs, though not the bed bug as some say. It is a bat bug, which has no interest in human beings, but of course would be unpleasant to have around.

We watched our colony of bats with interest. One day we found one clinging to a post in the boathouse. Close examination showed it to be a mother bat carrying a young one. There just couldn't have been a cuter sight than that. The little fellow was cuddled up to the mother's breast, both looking like very tiny monkeys with wings.

The Sausage family, our over-population of woodchucks, was staying on the island so far. They showed no tendency to spread out, but individual characteristics were becoming more plain. Link Sausage, the mother, was forcing the youngsters to depend on themselves. Self-sufficiency is a law for them, just as it is for us.

Thuringer seemed to take his schooling best. He was a quiet, studious type of creature who mixed little in family quarrels, and went about his way alone. To a degree Bratwurst got over the irritable disposition he first displayed. In fact, he became so obedient and docile we rather wished we hadn't chosen such an uncomplimentary name. Salami was still the jitterbug and getting worse. Ground hogs are serious-minded as a rule, but Salami would rather play than eat. She didn't want to play alone either. Much to their discomfiture, she was always trying to get her brothers to leave their food and play with her. She made herself most unpopular. Wiener was sort of a shy little fellow and often missing in the family circle.

Only on three occasions did we see all six of the young together. They certainly presented an amusing picture.

A woodchuck sits upright, like a prairie dog, and holds his food in his front feet. Thus he can look around for approaching danger while he nibbles away. Giny and I will long remember the way our Sausage family looked one morning when we put out a great quantity of carrots. There was so much food that for a few moments they forgot to fight. Patty the runt and O. Bologna the smart alec sat side by side looking something like Mutt and Jeff. It wasn't often that they were so peaceful. Sometimes I think Patty just loved the attention of being beaten by O. Bologna. He was always near the big brother, and regularly got into trouble. But now, for the moment, they were preoccupied with this luscious food. We have noticed that when they sit in a group this way, they all face different directions. No doubt this is so that they can watch more thoroughly for enemies. Such alertness was in evidence that day when the six of them were feasting on carrots.

Even as we watched them, laughing at their frantic and funny way of chewing, one of them gave a shrill whistle. The others dropped their carrots. Everyone was on the alert. All action was suspended for just an instant and then the same one repeated his warning. From overhead came the excited cry of More-Mo. Still-Mo echoed it from a distant tree. Something unusual was afoot on the island. Several woodchucks then joined in their sharp whistle of alarm—and that was enough. There was a fierce scramble for safety. Four of them tried to go in one hole at the same time! They squealed and scratched, and in some miraculous way managed to vanish into their underground homes.

Giny and I waited and watched. The red squirrels increased their scolding. Whoever the visitor was, he certainly was unwelcome from their viewpoint. Soon we saw a little motion in the brush, as something touched the bushes. Then came a sight that brought from us exclamations of both admiration and pity. A very young raccoon walked into full view. To see such a creature in full daylight was unusual in itself, but there was even more to explain about this little fellow. His walk was very unsteady, as if from exhaustion or some other cause he was hardly able to take another step. When he stopped, held his nose up in the air and sniffed in true raccoon style, he swayed as if about to fall over. His fur was extremely light in color as is sometimes the case when an animal is undernourished. His eyes seemed to be sightless.

"Oh, the poor little thing!" Giny exclaimed. "What is the matter with him? What is he doing here in the daytime? Do you suppose we can get some food to him?"

It wouldn't be too easy. The tiny creature was fearful and sensitive to noises. When we moved our feet just a little he made a pitiful attempt to run, though his flight ended when he fell to the ground after taking about a dozen steps. Plainly the animal was in trouble and needed help.

Giny warmed some milk, crumbled some bread into it and quietly placed it on the ground a few feet from where he still lay. We watched from our window to see what he would do. Apparently he caught the odor of the food. One halting step at a time, he approached the pan. His manner of eating suggested that something might be wrong with his mouth. I wondered if he might have got mixed up with a porcupine and had some quills imbedded in his tongue or nose.

We never learned the nature of his trouble. He became an established member of the island colony. Giny named him *Racket,* presuming that he was from the lineage of Rack and Ruin. He made his home under our cabin. For days after his arrival, feeding and protecting this little thing was one of our main interests.

The experience gave us much to think about. What had led this animal when ill and unable to care for himself in the forest to seek our island—the only place in the whole community where he would be safe from other creatures which might seek to destroy him, and where he would be cared for? How had he come? What had happened to his mother that she did not guard over him? Why did he trust us as he did increasingly as days went on?

Some of these questions were answered by later experience; some of them never were. A deep mystery remained about Racket. All we could do for him was keep food available and protect him. We did this, and so added to our Sanctuary experiences a very precious chapter.

X

A GOAD FROM SANDY

THE next letter we received from Sandy the Squoip was charged with so much enthusiasm and anticipation it would hardly stay in the envelope. Sandy was coming to the States! He didn't know when he would land, and couldn't have told us if he did know—but he was coming. He was still in the hospital when he wrote but he said, "They are sending me back to get rid of me. I am simply a blamed nuisance. Don't know what to do with myself, so I just get in everyone's hair. I am so healthy they don't want to let me out on the street, because I make everyone else look sick. No sense in my being here anyway and there never was. The damage was done to the jeep, not to me. I wrinkled up one of its fenders and it didn't even muss my hair."

Sandy said he would have about sixty days' leave. He wanted to spend some of it with us, and the rest with his folks and friends in their northern Minnesota town. "Then we go on for the big show in Asia," he said. "Some of the boys think we have had enough, but I don't. While there is a war going on, I want to be in it. I'll be ready if only I can get some of that good old northwoods air in my lungs, look at a sky that doesn't have a plane in it, and be free of crowds of people just for a little while.

I'll bet they put us in a slow old tub to go across the pond. Anything would seem slow to me when I am coming home. If I had Buddie here, I would start out now. By the way, do you still plan on finding Sanctuary Lake? I have been wondering if we might take a look around the canoe country during my furlough. Just an idea. Maybe it's all wet, but you can't blame a fellow for trying."

Giny and I looked at each other as we read this part of the letter aloud. The idea certainly was persistent. It kept prodding us all the time, and was working at Sandy too.

"Remember, we haven't any gas coupons for such a trip!" Giny insisted, following our usual routine.

"Sandy would be allowed some," I suggested.

"Our tires are rather thin," Giny went on in her practical way, "and the government does not want us to use cars for such purposes."

"Yes, I know." I shook my head to dismiss the whole proposition. "Then Buddie is hardly equal to it. We couldn't just choose smooth waters up there, and there are rocks barely under the surface of the lakes that might poke their heads up through one of the canoe's weak places. Anyway," I went on, satisfied that the impracticality of this ambition was established, "constant handling of the old canoe on portages would simply tear it apart."

"We could rent a canoe." Now Giny tried to insert a ray of hope.

"Sandy wouldn't like that. I believe he would rather

stay here and use Buddie in a limited way than to travel in a strange canoe. You know how sentimental he is about such things."

"Like ourselves!" Giny agreed. "All right, we won't count on it."

Sandy concluded his letter with the promise to wire us as soon as he had landed and could make definite plans.

I walked down to the canoe rack where Buddie lay covered with a canvas. I inspected the hull carefully for signs of weakness. The places I had fixed were holding well. I turned the canoe upright, and tested the rails. My mind was filled with memories and dreams. I pictured the portage from Sunday Lake into Meadow Lake, the campsite at the far end of Louisa—portages, streams, rapids and still more portages. Of all the joys the forest has offered me, canoe travel rates supreme. It gives the thrill of wilderness, the spice of variety, a challenge to strength and initiative, the poetic beauty of camp life.

Buddie in its best days was a fine canoe for such adventure. I pictured where the packsacks would fit. Buddie was seventeen feet long and of wide beam; it could carry the three of us and our supplies. Of course, every canoe traveler knows that the success of such a trip depends largely on the strength and vitality of his canoe. It is rather a serious predicament to be in to have the canoe itself go wrong in some remote spot in the Canadian canoe country. The country is of such nature that there is no other way to travel, except by plane.

Skeptically I fastened to Buddie the yoke by which it is carried. This would be quite a test, for the yoke clamps to the railings, placing upon them a great strain. I lifted the canoe to my shoulders and walked a few feet. There were sounds of stress, but not as bad as I had expected. It might possibly get by, I thought. But of course, there were the gas problem and the tires.

XI

BLESSED NOOTHANTH

Hi-Bub caused me to live in a quandary. For nearly a week we heard nothing of him. At first I was afraid he would come, then I was afraid he wouldn't. There were lots of things to be done and he was anything but a big help. However, my thoughts held to that lisp of his, his keen childish interest in the world about him, his three-shift imagination, his smile that rolled back his plump cheeks, and the twinkle in his eyes—and I began to feel that looking on such things was more important than doing a lot of chores. Then, too, Giny had not met him as yet, a deficit in experience that was charged directly against me.

One warm, still morning I was near the boathouse working at the endless job of repairing Buddie. A new break in the veneer had occurred, and although it was small it had to be fixed before it grew worse.

Sound carried well that morning. From away out to the west I could hear crows arguing. Blue jays gossiped incessantly. Then there came a thin little voice, plainly audible, from the nearest point on the mainland. I stopped my work, chuckled a little, and then listened. "Peanut-th!" came the cry. "Peanut-th!"

I slipped along the shore line and peered through some brush in the direction from which the sound had come. There stood Hi-Bub crying his wares. Stubby and Nuisance were being called—but he wasn't really looking for them. He was directing his voice right toward our island.

"Peanut-th! Peanut-th!" he called, so loudly his voice broke. Obviously Bub wanted some attention.

I stepped into the open. "Hi, Bub!" I greeted him.

"What?"

"I said 'Hi, Bub.'"

"Can't hear," he insisted.

"I said hello. You know, 'Hello!'"

"Ith Th-tubby over there?" he asked, ignoring my greeting.

Then followed a conversational confusion that probably resembled the jabbering at the Tower of Babel. We both talked at once, our *whats* clashed with our statements, and echoes mixed into everything said. We were getting nowhere in this long-distance communication. Hi-Bub couldn't understand a thing I said—at least not until I shouted, "Do you want to come over?"

"Huh?" he asked, listening for the first time.

"Do you want to come over to the island?"

"Oh, I don't care." Which was the embarrassed boy's way of saying, "Hurrah, that is what I have been working for!"

I took a rowboat and went over to get the young man, bag of peanuts, lisps, enthusiasm, imagination and all. It was high adventure for him, this trip in a boat, though he was careful not to let it seem too important or unusual. He had been in boats "lot-th of time-th!" he insisted. His daddy, who was a very remarkable person, I was coming to understand, had a submarine—just think of that! I thought, here we go again.

"Did you bring your submarine up here?" I asked, hoping to find out if the ship were fabricated entirely out of imagination, or if it were an inflated toy.

"No-o-o-o!" Bub was highly disgusted. Why that submarine was bigger'n this lake. Where was it? Why it was in the ocean, of course, right where his daddy had left it. Daddy, it seems, had been away off "after the Japth," and he had "Th-hot 'em all to pietheth." Apparently all the bullets hadn't gone one way and so Daddy was no longer of any use to the Navy. He had come home to stay. But I realized this was not a tall tale. Daddy *had* a submarine, at least an interest in one that was real and tangible.

We were nearing the island now, and Bub was looking about excitedly. He expected the place to be crawling with animals like some glorified zoo. I explained to him that our wildwood friends come at different times, some in the day, some in the night, that they are too busy living just to sit around the island waiting for callers. He hardly listened to me, becoming greatly excited over a grackle that perched on our boathouse. He might see a hundred such birds any day in a city park, but this one was simply wonderful because it was on our island.

Giny was there waiting for us. She had heard our voices and came to welcome our young guest.

"Hi-Bub, this is Mrs. Campbell," I said.

"Hello, Bub," said Giny, helping him from the boat. "Welcome to our island. How are you?"

Bub's manners were good. He took Giny's hand, smiling his best, and managed to assure her, "I'm thwell! How are you Mithuth Cammel?"

"I'm swell too, Bub," she said, then added to the boy's delight, "I think we are going to be friends for a long time, so suppose you just call me Giny, it will be easier."

Bub murmured something about Mithuth Giny, but his attention was directed elsewhere—in fact to many elsewheres. Still-Mo had come racing up, and Bub's sack of peanuts had to be opened in a hurry and a contribution made. More-Mo came also and the two red squirrels staged a little fight to the accompaniment of Hi-Bub's giggles. Chipmunks and blue jays came in numbers. Bub stood in the midst of a three-ringed circus, every event polished up to the peak of importance by his overactive imagination. This was an enchanted island to him.

Giny and I laughed uninterruptedly at the youngster. His enthusiasm stirred our own to greater volume. Our little island friends had never been ordinary to us, but it did add to our joy to see someone else loving them so much. Giny named each creature that came up, and Hi-Bub repeated the names, getting them all mixed up, mispronouncing them, but having a wonderful time.

"I-th thith a canoe?" he asked, stopping suddenly in

the midst of his play with animals and looking up at Buddie.

"Yes, we call it Buddie," I explained.

"No-o-o-o."

"Yes-s-s-s," I insisted.

But Buddie was the name of his daddy's friend, Bub said.

"Well, you see Hi-Bub, Buddie is a name we may call any good pal, someone we are close to. This canoe is a good pal. We have lots of fun with it, so we call it Buddie."

Hi-Bub was examining the patches and we asked him not to pull them off. I had to tell him we were getting it ready for a soldier who was coming to visit. This never should have been started. It lead to one of the worst linguistic tangles I have ever heard. Bub was excited about the soldier. Apparently his little mind was filled with admiration for our war heroes. Who was this soldier? When would he come? Could he see him? What was his name? There is where I made my mistake. I should have named our coming guest John and let it go at that. But innocently I headed into some difficulty.

"We call him Sandy the Squoip," I said.

Bub looked at me with a startled expression. If I had begun suddenly to grow geraniums on my head, the effect would have been about the same. He dropped his bag of peanuts and clamped both hands over his mouth as if trying vainly to hold back an atom bomb of laughter. He bent and twisted in his unsuccessful attempt to control his mirth. Giny and I laughed both with him and at him. Presently he ceased his contortions and again asked what was the name of that tholdier.

"Sandy the Squoip," I confirmed.

"Oh-ho, ho, ho," he giggled, though the spasm wasn't quite as extreme this time. Then Hi-Bub tried to say the name, and threw us all in stitches. Thandy he said with pretty good success, but when it came to Squoip, he hardly got through at all.

"Th-quoi-woi-woi-woi——" he stammered on helplessly, finally looking up at me for assistance.

"Squoi—puh!" I said, with great emphasis on the final *p*.

"Thquoi—*puh!*" Bub followed with such fidelity and such energy that Still-Mo, who had been nuzzling the peanut bag, took the outburst personally and went scurrying away for dear life.

"Thandy the Th-quoi-puh!" was named and placed in our boy's mental world. Through the rest of the day at times we heard him practicing his pronunciation.

There was another adventure in the offing for Hi-Bub. It came attended with a shock and, to his first impression, an impending calamity. He wanted to see the woodchucks. Giny had something cooking which needed attention, so she told him to come along and she would show him where the Sausage family lived. She left him looking among the bushes for these new friends. I had stayed at the canoe to finish the patch started earlier.

Hi-Bub looked earnestly about. The Sausages were not in evidence though the red squirrels and chipmunks followed him everywhere. He climbed up on a little rise and looked on the far side. Here was a big hole in the ground and it entranced him. He went to the edge and stooped over to look in. As he did so, Link Sausage the mother chose that particular moment to stick her head out. It was too unexpected for Bub. Giny and I heard a cry of fright. We both came running and saw Hi-Bub tumbling over backward, calling for the assistance of the Army, Navy, Marine Corps—and his daddy too. Link must have looked as big as a bear to him. He had wanted to see a woodchuck, but not like that. Link was as frightened as he was, and darted back into the ground. It took Giny, me, Still-Mo, More-Mo and four chipmunks to quiet Bub. Finally we got him to understand that it wasn't a dinosaur he had seen, but just our homely old pet ground hog.

"That was Link Sausage, Bub," Giny said consolingly. "She wouldn't hurt you."

"Link Thauthage?" asked Bub through tears of which he was already somewhat ashamed.

"Yes, that was Link Sausage. Shall we go and see her again? I believe you frightened her."

After much coaxing Hi-Bub consented to go a step at a time back to the scene of his great fright. Giny had to hold one hand while I held the other as we advanced over the little hill. We looked down at the hole. Link was just peeking out again, very timidly, probably wondering what had gone haywire with the island Sanctuary. Giny and I realized something of the problems of diplomacy right then. Link looked skeptically at this small-sized human being who could let out such yells as to scare the life out of well-meaning folks. Hi-Bub tugged slightly at our hands as if he would not like to get too near to that ugly old creature that pokes its head out of the ground and makes faces at little boys. It was a difficult situation and shows just what fear can do. Here were two beings well prepared to be friends. But through misunderstanding, they couldn't trust each other. Bub sniffed and sniffed and tried to laugh, but didn't succeed very well. Link didn't even sniff, she just stared. Giny, always resourceful in such emergencies, went into the house and returned with a peace offering. There was a cooky for Hi-Bub and a carrot for Link.

"Link wants you to have this cooky, Bub," she said, offering it to him. "She says she is sorry that she frightened you."

Sniff, sniff—"Thorry too!" said Hi-Bub, doing his best to pull out of it.

We finally induced him to hold the carrot toward Link. It was an intense moment for both of them. Link came one cautious step at a time toward her most loved food. Bub held the carrot out, but with many a little nervous jerk indicating he would rather not. At last the good-will offering was accepted, and Bub laughed his delight. The final scene was a complete triumph for the peacemakers.

Boy and woodchuck sat side by side, he eating a cooky—maybe three or four—and the animal feasting fearlessly on delectable carrots.

All in all, it was a wonderful day for Bub. He stayed for lunch and through the afternoon. When we told him we wanted to get some lunch ready, he replied, "Yeth, I told Mom you would."

The little schemer!

Bub saw all the woodchucks that day. He saw Racket too, discovering the young raccoon high in a tree. The position of the animal was astonishing. He had wedged himself into a crotch, hanging as limp as a bag of meal.

We were a bit concerned lest he had become fastened there, and we stirred him up by shaking the tree. He moved a little, proving his freedom, then returned to his original position in the crotch showing that that was where he wanted to be. Racket was making progress. His walk was steadier, his actions stronger. He still had difficulty eating and we were not sure he could see—but there was improvement, and we were glad. It was mighty easy to love the little creature.

In late afternoon came Bub's most thrilling adventure. The weather was perfectly calm, so we bundled him in a life jacket and took him home by canoe. Giny paddled bow, I paddled stern, and Bub sat amidships on a cushion. I watched the little lad fall head over heels in love with Buddie. He sat quietly as we asked him to, but his attention whipped about eagerly. The trees along the shore, the perfect reflections through which we glided, the eagle that soared gracefully almost out of sight overhead—all engaged him.

Hold to it, Bub, I thought. This is something mighty valuable you are feeling now. If, in the years before you, you can be satisfied with these pleasures, much contentment and happiness will be yours. Seeking of pleasure can mislead you, little fellow. It does many people. We human beings are often so unwise in our play. But Nature will never let you down, Bub, unless you yourself fail to remain sensitive to its charms. Some of your fairies and brownies may disappear as you grow older. But nature has an unlimited store of blessings to share with you, something suitable for every age. Next will come education, some of which will be false or faulty. Wise ones will whisper of strange so-called pleasures, others will laugh at this simple way of living. But hold on, Hi-Bub, don't let the world snatch your treasure from you. Fight for your right to love the forest, and it will never fail you.

Bub's parents met us at their pier. "You have started him on the road to becoming a naturalist," said his daddy, when introductions had been completed. I commented that there was nothing I would rather give a child than the desire to learn and love this world.

Hi-Bub and his parents went into their cabin, but I'll wager there was little opportunity to eat at their dinner table that night. Bub had too much to tell.

XII

RATZY-WATZY

OLDER folk could note with much benefit the persistence and resourcefulness of children in accomplishing a purpose. Opposition that would discourage the adult merely fires the determination of the young mind. Perhaps this is again proof that until we are "as little children" we cannot enter the kingdom of harmonious living.

Hi-Bub reached the island one day by a new route, when all paternal and maternal wishes had opposed his coming. His parents were afraid he would become a nuisance, they told him, forgetting for the moment that the nuisance value of a youngster is one thing that endears him to us. That day Hi-Bub was *not* to come down the trail. Parental orders were clear and emphatic.

Bub was really an obedient child. Besides, when one is clever, why risk the penalties of insubordination? He sang and played about his own yard for a while, according to Daddy's report, which I got later. He built a little house in the sand at the lake shore, and upon inquiry said it was for a young woodchuck who couldn't dig his own home. Bub tucked leaves and grass into the home to make it comfortable for "Hamburger"—an attempt to relate his imaginary friend to the Sausages on the island. He had seen our woodchucks gathering up mouthfuls of nesting materials, and reasoned Hamburger should have the same luxury. He did not say why Hamburger could not do this work for himself. Maybe the invisible woodchuck had just received a manicure, and didn't want his fingernails to get as dirty as Bub's did in this construction work. Or perhaps it was just the difficulty that an imagined being has in moving things about in the material world. Whatever the reason, Bub made a fine house for Hamburger.

When Daddy or Mom came near this busy boy, they heard remarks unrelated to the building program, however. Hi-Bub worried for fear "Th-tubby and Noothanth wath hungry." Daddy was sure the animals would survive one day without his attention. But "Tham Cammel" might wonder why he didn't come, Hi-Bub worried. Daddy thought probably "Tham" would get along all right, too. The persistent Bub reminded them that I had told him he was a help, that when he saw something new about the animals at the Sanctuary I was anxious to hear of it. He was supposed to keep watching them all the time, so I would have a way of knowing everything that happened. This was largely true. I did learn much through the constant observation Bub gave to the island creatures. However, Daddy remained unimpressed. He couldn't believe that "Tham Cammel's" progress as a naturalist rested upon the shoulders of his chubby son.

Suddenly Hi-Bub broke out with an enthusiastic desire to go fishing. Daddy had wanted him to go often before. What father doesn't want to go fishing with his son? It is a period of intimate companionship unequaled in life's ordinary routine. No fatherly conference in a parlor can be as effective as the confidences which flow when Dad and the young punk sit at the back end of fishpoles in a boat. The usual barriers are gone. Talk comes freely. Many a portion of fine fatherly advice can be dealt out while bait is being put on a hook, or a flopping fish pulled in. Daddy's authority and importance are increased. His long experience in the science of fishing crowns him king for the nonce. This exalted position, based upon ability at angling, makes his opinion on other subjects savor of finality, the ultimate in wisdom. So it is that while Father and Son drift along trolling hopefully or watching a bobber record the nibbling of a perch, effective comments may be made upon the old telltale report card, or about dressing neatly, or perhaps being more polite and obedient to Mother.

Bub's daddy knew this, or at least instinctively felt it, and so he and Bub went fishing. Bub took the interwoven advice rather well, but he was an impatient fisherman. If one place did not produce a bite in a hurry, he wanted to move on. Maybe up ahead at that old log would be better—and Daddy would row thither. Or perhaps on by those lilypads would be a good spot. Place after place was tried, with varying success. Only the moving on was consistent.

Strangely the locations Bub selected were always in one direction—toward the Sanctuary. They worked along the shore line until the island was in view. Then Bub decided the one spot on earth where there would be "thwell fith" was right near our boathouse. He had seen them there—great big fish that were longer than he could stretch.

Daddy was getting suspicious, but he complied with the request. What else could he do? Over to the island they came, and dropped anchor a few feet offshore. The enormous fish Bub had pictured did not show up immediately. In fact, it was so shallow at this spot that even a good-sized rock bass would have had to crawl along the bottom to keep his dorsal fin submerged.

Hi-Bub was not watching his fishing now. His attention was directed toward the island. Little ailments began manifesting themselves. His old political cough was most aggressive and prominent. Even where I sat in the cabin at my typewriter, I could hear his repeated "Ah-hem!" He became awfully tired of the boat. The seat was too hard and a cushion did no good. He wanted a drink of water. He was hungry. He wanted to stand up and stretch—and of course he had been taught never to stand up in a boat. There was Still-Mo, and there was More-Mo, and there was a woodchuck he couldn't identify unless he was ashore. In fact it looked as if that one woodchuck was running away, and he thought he ought to tell "Tham Cammel." Daddy was weakening under the bombardment. About this time I came down to the boathouse, and the political cough broke out furiously.

"Hi, Bub!" I called, in full appreciation of the situation.

"Huh?" said Bub.

"We are doing a little fishing today," commented the father by way of greeting, but he didn't sound convinced or convincing.

"So I see," I called back. "Any luck?"

There was a further exchange of conversation, all of which was much beside the point. Hi-Bub wanted out on that island! Would I mind if he got a drink? Of course not. Conveniently I suggested maybe he would want to stay ashore for a while to rest. Daddy could go on fishing if he wished, and I suggested some likely spots I know rather well. Daddy let Hi-Bub out, flashing a wink at me.

"I have a sneaking hunch that this is what he has been fishing for all the time," he said wisely.

Bub objected to the insinuation with one of his long drawn out "No-o-o-o's." However, as Daddy started to pull away, the boy called frantically for him to wait a minute. He went to the bow of the boat and from hiding drew forth his brown sack filled with peanuts!

"Now why did you bring those along on a fishing trip?" asked Daddy with an accusing look.

"Oh—'cause!" said Bub. And I guess that is explanation enough for anyone.

We had been hoping especially for a visit by Bub that day. There were goings on at the island. Another new member had joined our colony. We knew at dawn that the newcomer wasn't overly welcome. The woodchucks went about their business in the usual way, apparently with no concern, but the squirrels were much excited. Still-Mo scolded incessantly. More-Mo raced from one tree to another, turning his head this way and that intently observing something on the ground. He was highly curious and mystified. Whatever it was obviously was new to him. We saw a little motion in the grass and realized it must be a rather small animal that was causing this commotion. Giny caught a fleeting glimpse of it, learning that its color was a mousy gray. It took a lot of tiptoeing around and quiet observation before we caught full view of the newcomer. Then we discovered that we had acquired a wood rat!

Now please don't feel too horrified until we understand things better. I know a rat is less loved than anything other than a snake. But there are different kinds of rats just as there are different kinds of people. We would be unwise to think all mankind is evil because a Hitler appears in our midst. There have been Lincolns and Washingtons too, to give us a better idea of the true human nature. There are house rats, and I know of nothing to say in their defense. They are the lowest and most threatening form of animal life, viewed from the standpoint of human welfare. But such species as the muskrat and the wood rat are vastly different from the kind that pester our cities. The wood rat that had come to our island was a creature of clean habits, and intelligent, interesting ways. One may be somewhat shocked to hear it, but the flesh of this animal is considered by woods dwellers as good to eat, in fact superior to that of many other so-called game animals. Generally he lives in a clean home under the ground. His food consists almost exclusively of grains, grasses and seeds. He stores up food for winter, as does the squirrel. He does not carry disease or vermin. He is pleasant to look at—that is, if we have smothered our prejudice—and his ways are wise, cute and friendly.

Giny wasn't very pleased at first when I announced that our guest was a rat. It took a lot of explaining. She would not hurt any creature under the sun, but she was inclined to seek methods of colonizing this fellow elsewhere. However, I shared my knowledge of his kind with her, and we gained additional information by looking into our nature books. We watched the animal working at his problems, noted the rich beauty of his coat and his odd little mannerisms. Soon we were laughing at him. Then we sympathized with him. At last, after several hours, we had accepted him as a part of this endless drama going on about us. In him we saw one more opportunity to study the social system of the forest, and to learn how this animal fits in with those among whom he must live. Then we gave him a name! We called him "Ratzy-Watzy," and from that moment on he was important to us.

When Hi-Bub arrived, the interest in Ratzy-Watzy was still new and at its peak. The boy had no prejudice to overcome. He had a little trouble saying Ratzy-Watzy, but he had no difficulty in loving the strange animal. We brought Bub up to the minute on what had happened.

The attitude of the squirrels toward this rat was one of the most amusing things I have watched in the forest. Undoubtedly they were uncertain as to what he was, what he could do, how fast he could move, and just how tough he could be. He fed on the grain we had placed on the ground for other animals, so he was a rival. He needed to be scolded. I think a large measure of a squirrel's scolding is like whistling in the dark anyway. The creature jabbers to bolster up its own courage. More-Mo would sit on a limb twenty feet above where Ratzy-Watzy was eating and rant and rail at him. The rat would make no reply, but would look up as much as to say, "Says you!"

Then the squirrels began deliberately to test the rat for courage and speed. They discovered the tiny gray creature was rich in the former and lacking in the latter. He met the challenge of the chickarees with utter defiance. He made no sound that we could hear, but by his attitude indicated that he wouldn't back up a step for the whole tribe of red squirrels. He went up to the foot of the tree where More-Mo bombarded him with insults, and reached up his front feet as if he would like to come up there and pull out every red hair, one at a time. But he couldn't climb!—and that was an important discovery for More-Mo. From then on the squirrels became bolder and bolder. More-Mo came down the trunk of the tree head first until he was within two feet of the ground, and there he hung, increasing his loud banter. It was getting the best of Ratzy-Watzy. He tried vainly to reach More-

Mo. He even jumped in his direction, but it was a clumsy, unavailing effort. More-Mo merely chattered louder than ever.

Things were at this stage when Hi-Bub joined us. The whole thing made a terrific impact on his imagination. He began to tell us that "he had a rat one-th." Of course it was a bigger rat that lived in his icebox, and used to follow him to school. We would have been interested to hear the story of that remarkable animal, except the creatures outside our cabin were beginning a new phase of experience. Bub forgot the icebox rat to watch and laugh at what he saw.

Still-Mo and More-Mo had joined forces against Ratzy-Watzy. Like a family row that settles itself quickly when an outsider intervenes, these two forgot their own differences before the invader. They tormented and teased that rat in a planned and systematic way that finally drew our sympathy to the side of Ratzy-Watzy. Never did they allow him a moment's rest. One or the other or else both chickarees were at him constantly. They had learned that they could make three moves while he made one. They could outrun him without half trying, they could dodge him so skillfully that he looked silly, and the supreme thing in their favor was he couldn't climb a tree.

Apparently they respected the rat's prowess. They would not engage him in combat. Theirs was a war of attrition and the rat fell for their little game. He simply could not ignore their teasing. It would have been wiser had he held to his eating, closed his ears to their jibing and just been ready to repel any direct attack. But he had to chase them, and that was just what they wanted. Back and forth we saw them go, Ratzy-Watzy the pursuer, Still-Mo or More-Mo the pursued. The squirrels were not trying to get away, they were just making him come on. Their pace was much slower than normal. They wanted to keep close enough so he would think there was a chance of catching them. If he stopped for a moment, they stopped too. In fact, when he remained quiet too long, probably out of breath, a red squirrel would make a run at him and jump completely over his head. No self-respecting wood rat could stand that, of course, and he would take up the chase again. It actually looked pitiful to see one of the squirrels go bouncing along, spritely as a spring wind, and then lumbering, awkward old Ratzy-Watzy come laboring after him, mad as a hornet but helpless.

The chase went on for hours. We turned to other things,

but whenever we looked out, there was Ratzy-Watzy chasing either Still-Mo or More-Mo.

The chickarees were now working shifts on him. The climax of the ordeal came about the time Hi-Bub's daddy was calling from the boathouse that they must go home. Giny went down and persuaded him to come up to see this strange drama.

The scene of the conflict now centered about a great white pine tree which stands within view of our window. More-Mo was leading the luckless rat around and around the base of the tree. Dizziness was being added to Ratzy-Watzy's weariness. Gamely he trudged along, but he never came close to his tormentor. In fact, More-Mo had developed the utmost disrespect for him. Several times during this circling about the tree, the squirrel suddenly reversed his direction, came head on at the surprised rat and jumped lightly over his head. Then the chase went on in the other direction for a while. Ratzy-Watzy was nearing the end of his endurance; More-Mo was as fresh—and fresh is the word for it—as he had been at the beginning of the day.

The rat stopped suddenly, actually lying down. More-Mo mounted the tree and came within a few inches of the rat's nose, chattering at him insultingly, probably saying something like, "Yah, you ain't so tough. Who'd you think you're chasing around? Come on, funny face, let's have fun." The rat roused himself and lunged at the squirrel, but More-Mo avoided him and started around the base of the tree again. Around and around in one direction, then around and around in another, until Giny burst forth, "Now that is just plain cruel. I'm going to get Ratzy-Watzy some food and keep those squirrels away from him until he can eat."

But the tormented creature sought his own rest. He went across the ground at a pace that indicated near exhaustion, and disappeared under a shed. More-Mo chattered a laugh after him, and lightly ran to the top of a tree.

"I'm glad you called me up," Bub's daddy said. "If I had been told about this, I probably would have thought it was just another one of those things!" He looked askance at Bub.

Hi-Bub's powers of observation were much keener than ours, we discovered. As he and Daddy rowed away to complete their "fishing trip," we heard him talking in a loud, excited way, words getting all mixed up with each other, telling a score of wonderful things Ratzy-Watzy had done that we never saw at all.

XIII

HORIZONS AND HOPES

IT WAS one of those unseasonably cold summer evenings that nature loves to weave into the rugged plan of the north country. Rain had fallen from a solid gray sky throughout the day. The persistent drops became fewer as the afternoon waned, and at twilight hour they ceased, leaving the forest cold and dripping. At the horizon in the northwest the vast cloud parted, slowly lifting like a great curtain. Golden shafts of sunlight played through the opening, high-lighting hilltops, painting the under parts of the cloud curtain with regal splendor.

By the time darkness ruled, the sky was clear, night air was chilled and pleasant to breathe, and stars sparkled as if washed of all cosmic dust by the rain.

"It seems something should be done with a night like this," Giny said, as we looked from our windows at the inviting beauty.

"Any suggestions?" I asked.

"Yes. How about climbing to the top of Brown Hill?"

To Brown Hill we went, first crossing the lake by canoe, and then following a trail that we knew even in utter darkness. Saplings playfully showered us with raindrops they had collected, wayside brush bathed us with moist branches, and grasses washed our feet as we walked along.

Boots and raincoats kept us dry, however, and we continued our journey to the hilltop—the highest point in our Sanctuary.

As we looked down into tree-filled valleys, now dimly lighted by starlight, we noted tiny little curls of vapor rising. The cold was having a magical effect. Fog was radiating from the comparatively warm earth, and rapidly engulfing the forest. Even as we watched, valleys were filled. In soft waves it rolled out across the lake. Within an hour the world beneath us seemed to have disappeared, and our little hilltop was an island in an infinite sea. Slight movements in the mass of fog gave us the feeling that we were afloat.

Then out of the east rose the evening star, sparkling energetically. Giny gazed intently at this new addition to our extravaganza.

"What are you thinking?" I asked, when it seemed that silence had reigned long enough.

"I was wondering about Sandy," she said.

"Yes?"

"He may be on a sea in the direction of that star—right now. He may be coming home, even as we stand here. You and I can only guess what it means to him, for we never were drawn so far from home, mentally and physically, as he has been. Wouldn't you like to know what he is thinking as he turns his back on that land which means only strife to him and heads for home and peace?" Giny was still watching the evening star as she talked, as though in its messages she could read Sandy's story.

Strangely, at that time our soldier was sailing the sea—at long last *coming home*. In weeks that followed when we visited with him and compared notes, we discovered that while we looked upon the loveliness of that fog-filled landscape, he was riding the ocean in the largest canoe he had ever seen. Every event on that journey made such an indelible impression on his memory that the story was still vivid when told to us.

His ship, we learned, was one of the largest in service. It plowed fearlessly the restless waters of the Atlantic, leaving a fading furrow through liquid hills. Sandy told how he "pulled bow paddle" as much as regulations would allow. He stayed where the spray broke upon his face with cooling, yet stinging effect. Always his eyes were glued on a distant horizon toward which the great craft traveled, though to appearances with never a yard of gain.

Sandy was lonely on that voyage, yet far from alone. Thousands of other lads rode the same super-canoe, each heart singing in its own original strain, "Going home, going home." Sandy felt little of their companionship. His mind was as much at sea as the ship on which he sailed. His thoughts were tossed about by alternating waves of memory, anticipation, uncertainty, hope and frustration. Sometimes there was a fear of what was ahead, and yearning for that which was behind, dreadful though it had been. In combat there were fear, discomfort and exhaustion beyond words. Yet, there was a freedom from responsibility. Mean as was that picture of life, it was all decided for him. All he had to do was go forward, take the objective military decision pointed out. Tomorrow was certain—it would bring more and more of the same thing without his planning or his initiative. He lived moment by moment; the hundred square feet of ground about him was his world. Nothing further on need concern him. There would be orders governing his moves and motives when another day came.

Now the future, symbolized in that dancing, ever-receding horizon, seemed a plastic to be molded by his own hands. Someday soon there would be no more military commands. Then his decisions would be his life. True, there was a war in the Pacific to be won. But there were rumors that it might end sooner than had been anticipated.

In his vacillating thought one instant he wished it were over and the next, although he would not admit such an idea even to himself, he wished he might get into it. At least, it would delay this coming responsibility.

Loved ones were awaiting him beyond that horizon. That was a happy thought, and his heart quickened under its influence. He remembered the home scenes, his family and friends, the things he had loved so much in those laughing days of youth. Pictures paraded through his mind. He could see the very street on which he had lived. His town was small, and the forest came right up to the outskirts. There were boyhood fishing adventures, camping experiences, the "old gang" of associates who shared the everyday hours, school—all revolving about a firm, comfortable home that stood atop a small hill.

While Sandy was slow in admitting it, we learned that there were sly tears coursing down his cheeks during such meditation. Home thoughts were harder on the eyes than the salty ocean breeze.

He told that a deep voice spoke behind him saying, "Not all the battles are at the front, are they, soldier?" He looked around to see a Chaplain smiling sympathetically, as if understanding all that was going on in Sandy's mind.

"No, sir," said Sandy the Squoip, embarrassed and striving to hide his emotion.

"Anything you want to talk over with me, lad?" asked the Chaplain, examining with appreciation the service ribbons on Sandy's breast.

Sandy was getting control of his voice. "No, sir," he said, now really smiling. "It's nothing. I'm just getting soft, I guess."

The Chaplain laughed aloud. "When a man has the courage to earn this," he said, pointing to Sandy's medal, "and still has the fineness of character to shed those—" now he pointed to the tears persisting in the soldier's eyes—"then he is a bit of all right in here." The Chaplain slapped with the back of his hand over Sandy's heart.

The tall blond boy could only smile in reply, and the Chaplain started to walk away with a final "Good luck, soldier, keep your shoulders square." However, he turned suddenly and came back.

"I found something in my copy of Emerson that is pretty good medicine, soldier. Want to hear it?" he asked, taking a small notebook from his pocket. Sandy did.

" 'How dear, how soothing to man, arises the idea of God, peopling the lonely place, effacing the scars of our mistakes and disappointments!' Like it?" The sentence was read with warm enthusiasm and appreciation.

The tall soldier repeated the words as if trying to engrave them in his memory. " 'How dear, how soothing to man, arises the idea of God, peopling the lonely place, effacing the scars of our mistakes and disappointments!' " The Chaplain prompted him when necessary, but Sandy had caught the message very well.

"Like it?" persisted the Chaplain.

"Yes, sir—I sure do!" affirmed Sandy. "It asks a lot of a fellow, though."

"Offers him a lot, too," added the other, turning a page in his notebook. "Now add this to it: 'He is sure that his welfare is dear to the heart of being . . . he believes that he cannot escape from his good.' "

Sandy found a ray of hope in the words, but there was also a question. "But, sir, how do you take a thing like that in?" he asked. "I like the words, like the idea, but how do you eat it up, digest it, and make it yourself?"

The Chaplain laughed. "Take a big bite and keep chewing, Sergeant," he said, turning to leave once more. "It's sort of heavy food, but it's packed with nourishment—and God made you able to take it!"

It was two days later when the strong, proud skylines of New York stood boldly against the western sky. Sandy was at the bow, looking toward it with conflicting emotions. He wondered at himself. Through weeks of anticipation he had imagined what this moment would be like. With his buddies he speculated on what he would do. There was always the suggestion of hilarity. They would turn handsprings! They would yell until their voices could be heard in the old home town! They would be so wild with joy, anything might happen—they might even dive in the ocean and swim on ahead of the ship. No such things occurred. A few soldiers shouted in a half-hearted way but most of them stood, as did Sandy, just looking ahead and thinking. The joy they had anticipated was there, but it came with sobering effect.

"If it hadn't been for the other fellows, I would have

dropped to my knees," Sandy said of this solemn moment. "And I really believe they all wanted to do it, too!"

Sandy walked down the gangplank, his mind in a whirl of tangled thoughts. He tried to recall the quotation the Chaplain had given him, but couldn't get it right. Promising that he would look it up sometime, he lost himself in military problems of the moment.

XIV

INKY!

A LETTER told us of Sandy's landing and of his plans. The usual military uncertainty was in the background, but he had learned approximately the date on which his furlough was to begin and had figured out the time to the minute when he expected to arrive at the Sanctuary.

"I want to see little things!" Sandy had written, underscoring the word little with several lines. "I am tired of big ones. I want a little canoe instead of a big ship. I want a little cabin instead of a big barracks. I want a little group of friends in place of regiments. I am tired of big distances too. For as long as possible, I want to be in one little spot, read a little, hike a little, eat a little (but not too little!) and sleep a little."

"I wunner if he wanth a little boy, huh?" asked Hi-Bub, who was on a visit to the island when we read Sandy's letter.

Bub was very much excited about the coming of our soldier. Sandy, even in the abstract, was a tremendous hero to him. He had become fairly proficient at saying the name Squoip, and once in awhile tried desperately to go through the whole silly routine that had coined it.

Bub asked questions about Sandy until we ran out of answers. How tall was he? How old? How wide? How thick? How fast could he run and how high could he jump? He took to demonstrating how Sandy would charge at an enemy, and I had to call a halt to keep our island bushes from being trampled to earth. Woodchucks dived into fox holes and squirrels took to the tall trees before the frantic assaults of this one-Bub army could be stopped.

I tried to counter the idea of Sandy's military prowess by an account of how kind he was, and what a wide smile he flashed upon the world. It started Hi-Bub on a new theme. How wide was that smile? Was it this big?—and he looked up at me with a moderate grin on his face. Yes, it was fully as large as that! Then was it this big?—and he tugged frantically with the muscles at the corners of his mouth until two deep dimples were formed there, and his cheeks looked like McIntosh apples. Yes, it was even larger than that. Bub then launched a series of facial contortions that would have been frightening to anyone who didn't know the purpose. He pushed and tugged at his cheeks trying to make them get out of that super-smile's way. He caught the corners of his mouth with his fingers and pulled until he pushed his ears back, making himself look like the top man on a totem pole. In the midst of this mangling maneuver there would come a jumble of sounds resembling a phonograph when it is running down, but no doubt meaning, "Ith Thandy's thmile thith big?" I assured him that at last he had reached the record-breaking proportions of the soldier's famous grin. That ended it, but Hi-Bub's cheeks and lips were red for an hour from the punishment they had taken.

The situation next produced a spell of gambling in Hi-Bub. Sandy evolved into a veritable Paul Bunyan. Bub placed bets on him with unwavering faith. "I bet Thandy could lift that canoe with one hand," declared Bub. He bet that Sandy could walk "a hunnerd mileth." He bet the soldier could eat more bark than Inky. The volume of the gambling was staggering. Bub bet a million dollars "Thandy" could lift a certain log which I told him five men couldn't move. He bet another million his hero could skin a bear alive. The only way I could think of to end this gambling spree was to tell Hi-Bub that Sandy the Squoip never bet.

"I bet he duth!" said the irrepressible Bub.

There was new adventure in the air as we took Hi-Bub home that day. The waters were a glassy calm, so we launched Buddie for the trip. Bub had been told that we were being careful of the old canoe so it would be at Sandy's service when he arrived. Thereafter the boy treated it as tenderly as if it were a bubble. He cautioned me to be careful as I slipped it into the water. If his hero loved that canoe that was enough for Bub. The most important thing in the world right then was that no harm, not even a fingernail scratch, must be on the craft. As we moved out into the lake, Giny in the bow and Bub sitting on the deck all wrapped up in a life jacket, he told me I'd better be careful and not bump the side of the canoe with my paddle. He suggested to "Mithuth Cammel"—very politely of course—that she had better not move her feet around, it would scratch the varnish. Buddie had suddenly acquired a most vigilant guardian.

We moved along in silence now, close to shore where the low limbs of trees made us stoop occasionally to pass beneath them, and the graceful branches of loosestrife brushed against the canoe. White water lilies were in bloom and we drifted near to look into their colorful cups and catch their sweet scent. Wild roses smiled out at us from the water's edge, and little clusters of wild iris added their orchidlike beauty to the summer scene. Out in the open lake a dozen baby mallard ducks sailed away from us, convoyed by the proud mother. Hi-Bub wasn't supposed to talk, that was our agreement, but he pointed so strenuously he jolted the canoe. The ducks swam faster and faster, and Bub put them to full flight with his laugh that begins with a *whe-e-e* and ends with a *hick*.

There came a "sh-h-h-h" from Giny. Something was moving about on the shore. We could hear dry leaves being pushed about and crushed, and occasionally there was the crackling of a twig. We ceased our paddling and drifted. Hi-Bub had been taught always to remain still in a canoe, and like the true little woodsman he was, he held to this instruction now, but he was nearly bursting with anticipation. The old canoe behaved in that marvelous way we had seen throughout its years of service. It glided on steadily, slowly, silently. There was the whisper of lilypads brushing against its side, but no other sound. The creature in the brush continued to move about, slowly making its way in our direction.

Then into view not fifty feet from us came a grizzled old porcupine! Giny gasped a little, so did I. I whispered another "sh-h-h-h" toward the vibrant Bub. He looked as if he were about to explode.

Seeing a porcupine was a part of almost every hike, ride or canoe trip about our Sanctuary. But there was something unusual in this adventure. This was not just a porcupine—it was a particular one. The dignity of years rested upon the creature. He was huge for his kind, probably as large as a porky ever gets. His quills and hair were toned with gray. Cautiously he looked about, then with measured stride he moved toward the water.

"Sam, do you suppose it could be—?"

Giny never finished her question. The old porky had discovered us, now thirty feet from him due to the drifting of the canoe. He rose on his hind feet and shook out his quills. He turned as if to make his escape, then halted and regarded us again. With deliberation he raised his head and into the still air gave the porcupine call.

"Honk, honk, honk!" he went in slow cadence and descending tone, though I think his words would be more nearly correct in spelling if we left off the "k."

Giny replied to him in perfect mimicry. The three of us sat entranced, Giny and I under the spell of thoughts not yet shared with Hi-Bub. This old creature on the shore—his size, his obvious age, his call—could it be the one we hoped it was? The next few moves would tell.

Giny called again, and I added some comments in porky tongue. The animal looked at us curiously. He had some things to decide too. Our identity was important to him. Not all of those two-legged animals were the same. Some of them might be trustworthy, but others would just as soon shoot a fellow as not.

"Honk, honk, honk," pleaded Giny. "Oh, Sam, it must be he—it must be!" She moved about in violation of the instructions given Hi-Bub, causing the canoe to tilt and send little wavelets from its sides out through the reflections.

"Don't th-cratch Buddie!" whispered Hi-Bub.

On the shore there was action that was convincing and gratifying. The old porcupine abandoned all caution. Talking in little murmurs, he walked in his awkward way right toward us. Giny could restrain herself no longer.

"Inky!" she called. "Inky! Oh, Sam, get me in there. It *is* Inky!"

I needed no such orders. Already the bow of the canoe was being guided into the shore. Giny was out as soon as it touched, in spite of Bub's caution to be careful of the varnish. Bub and I followed with as much rapidity as debarking from a canoe permits. Giny was already kneeling beside the porcupine. No question in the world but that it was our old pet. No one had seen him in a year. Yet he knew us and reached up his front paws to us just as he had when he was a youngster. That was over seven years ago when Inky had been brought to us, then three days old. We had reared the odd little creature in our cabin. His sense of humor, his pranks, his intelligence had enriched our experience during the months and years that followed. When liberated in the forest, the wilderness had claimed him. We saw less and less of him. The previous summer one of our guests had seen him, but we had missed him. Hence, it was two years since this old fellow had laid eyes on us.

Undoubtedly Inky was glad to see us! He sniffed at our fingers, and permitted us to stroke his head, talking his little porky language all the while. In his early years he had formed a very annoying habit of locking his legs about my shin and pretending he was going to bite the skin off just as he does the bark of a tree. Now he tried this again. It was a fading impulse. With just a flash of youthful energy he grasped my leg with his front paws. He turned his head sideways as if to take a bite. Then with a little grunt that seemed to say, "Aw, here I am trying to act like a kid at my age," he sat down on the ground again. The gesture delighted us.

In the excitement of the moment I forgot our little boy. When I looked around I saw him standing in one of those comas of amazement that we had seen before. It was the way he had looked that first day he came across the trail and I suddenly appeared before him. All he could do was stand, stare, and say, "Oh-h-h-h!" Here was another of those utterly unbelievable things. He had heard of the famous Inky. He had read of him, and seen him in motion pictures. In fancy he had met him on the trails, and Inky had chased bears away from him—remember? But here before him was Inky himself! It was almost too much. Bub's eyes were like dinner plates, blue ones of course, and he forgot even to wink.

"Hi-Bub," I said to him, trying to stir him out of his trance, "this is Inky—you know Inky, the porcupine!"

"Oh-h-h-h!" said Bub, not twitching a muscle.

"Yes," I assured him, "this is Inky. Come on up and pet him. He won't hurt you. Come on!"

Bub had to be led; he couldn't travel under his own steam. He might have been able to endure the sudden appearing of fairies, but to have Inky the porcupine within sight and within reach—he could hardly take it in. I took his hand and maneuvered him a step at a time over to Inky. His little fingers finally touched timidly the porcupine's nose and brushed lightly over the rough coating of quills. Ultimately Hi-Bub was lisping short sentences to the porcupine patriarch, and mixing in his special laugh of delight.

There was a limit to Inky's endurance of us. Likely we would have stayed beside him for hours had he permitted it. But he had more to do than indulge sentimental meetings over-long. There was a lot of chewing to be done back in the forest, a lot of trees to be climbed too. With definite purpose he suddenly turned away from us, stood on all fours, and shook out his quills. Grunting a little farewell, that likely had in it a request to go away and let him alone, he walked away at a steady but slow pace. We called our farewells to him.

Hi-Bub did more than that. He walked along with the old porky, now thoroughly companionable with the creature. He even pulled the brush to one side to make Inky's path smoother. The two disappeared over the top of a little knoll. A few minutes later, in response to our calls, the boy returned, the whole adventure having excited him so much his feet would barely touch the ground. Already his capable imagination was at work. He had seen a "mama porcupine with theven babies" waiting for Inky back on a log—which is doing right well since a porcupine is seldom if ever known to have more than one young. We took Hi-Bub on home, and I dare say his dinner table vibrated with talk about Inky that night. Assuredly, ours did.

XV

A TENT FOR TWO

JULY vanished over the horizon of time, and the strong sun of August played upon the north country. It was to be a month the nations will never forget. In its tandem of thirty-one days trooping single file through a bewildered world, were to be events that shook humanity to its foundation.

Into our private lives at the Sanctuary came experiences that likewise will never leave us. As for Hi-Bub, it would be well if he does not have to wade through such a month often. The strain might be too great.

To begin with, our tent house had been put in readiness for the arrival of Sandy the Squoip. This was a structure eight by twelve, made of canvas stretched over a light cabin framework. We had established it long ago as a residence for youthful visitors who came to take their fill of nature. This tent house made an inviting little place, and Hi-Bub eyed it covetously. His sly, calculated looks and questions kept up an incessant hinting. When had I said Sandy would come? He knew full well from oft repeating, but he wanted me to say it again. It would be in about a week. Well—who would be sleeping in that tent house with Sandy? No one, we informed him; we wanted Sandy to be perfectly free while his visit lasted.

Well—who would be sleeping in the tent house before Sandy came? No one, we said.

"It-th a big tent jutht to have no one in it," commented Hi-Bub.

"Who do you think should be in it, Hi-Bub?" I was catching on with my usual slowness.

"Gee-e-e," said Hi-Bub, looking at that mansion in canvas. "I never thlept inna tent!"

"Not even in the jungle?" I asked.

Bub ignored the reference, and continued to gaze at the tent house with mounting desire. I followed him as he walked over to the door and looked inside. There were two cots all made up with an abundance of covers, and it really looked mighty comfy and inviting. "Oh-h-h-h!" said Hi-Bub.

Bub surely had that knack of wanting something so desperately that you just had to give it to him. His little heart was doing double duty at the romance and adventure suggested by these primitive conveniences. The adhesion of a boy and a tent is almost as powerful as that of a boy and a dog. What youngster does not thrill at the thought of life under a canvas? In the idea are embodied exploration, life at the frontier, faraway places, and the pitting of himself against the world.

"I have an idea!" I said to Bub. He looked up at me with an expression that told me he had it too. He reminded me of a puppy who has been offered a bone and is now waiting upon its coming with every fiber alive with expectancy. Bub didn't say a word. He didn't need to.

He knew what I was going to say, and I knew he did.

"If your parents approve——" I began.

"Yeth!" said Bub. "I athked them and they thed I could."

"You could what?" I asked, remembering the first invitation to lunch.

"Thtay inna tent tonight!" said Bub.

"Well, you certainly save a lot of talk figuring out things in advance that way, young fellow," I said, a bit disconcerted. "Anyway, we had better go home and get your pajamas. You didn't bring them today, did you?"

"No," said Bub with disarming honesty. "I wuth goin' to, but I forgot."

During the afternoon we went for his pajamas, and for the permission of his parents, which I learned had already been granted—if I asked him to stay. But he wasn't to hint! Bub never hinted. He didn't even ask for those things which, in the highest sense, were due him. He was just so convinced that these most desired adventures were coming that they came.

I fixed up the extra cot in the tent for myself. Bub insisted that he wasn't afraid to stay alone, but silence is a pretty big thing, and northwoods nights can get very dark. While there is nothing that would harm him, a fertile imagination like his could make him rather miserable if he were left alone.

Giny had a story to tell us when we returned from our trip to Bub's home. There was much ado among the squirrels. She had heard More-Mo, Two-Mo and Still-Mo suddenly break out in fierce chattering. It was not the kind of call heard when some danger faced them. This was more the conversation of anger. She sought out the squirrels and found them racing wildly about in hot pursuit of a fourth squirrel that had appeared from somewhere. It was a merciless chasing. Still-Mo raced after the visitor, running him up and down trees and about the boathouse until he fled from her territory. Then Two-Mo made after him at high pace when he entered the region near the campfire site. Next More-Mo made life miserable for him in the cabin area.

There was a little lull in the battle when Bub and I arrived on the scene. It gave us a chance to identify the visiting squirrel. We found him seated breathless and exhausted in the top of a small wild cherry tree. I coaxed, and Bub coaxed, but the little creature wouldn't come down.

There was something very familiar about the tiny refugee. We examined him through binoculars, while from three directions we could hear the scolding of our inhospitable Still-Mo, More-Mo and Two-Mo. There was an unusually brilliant color to his back and tail. We strongly suspected that it was No-Mo, who had disappeared weeks before, and we were convinced of this identification when the creature gave in to the temptation of peanuts and came down from his lofty perch.

We were not the only ones watching him, however. No sooner had his feet touched the ground than both More-Mo and Still-Mo came running at him from two directions, and the chase was on again. It was anything but a

A TENT FOR TWO

hearty welcome to receive from his family. Blood relationship seemed to count for nothing. If the island squirrels had the least memory of this visitor, it was an unpleasant one. He was in their eyes simply an invader, a potential thief. Still-Mo had a fortune in various foods planted about the boathouse area. Two-Mo had equal wealth in her hollow oak tree, and in several score chosen spots in the ground. More-Mo had packed our attic with previous possessions gathered through hard labor. The visitor was a threat to all this. Their answer was to run after him incessantly, never giving him a moment's peace. Even Ratzy-Watzy took up the chase. No-Mo didn't have a spot on the island where he could rest, and not a friend who was in a position to help him, though certainly our sympathy was on his side.

We lectured the three hostile squirrels about their manners, and about a Christianly attitude toward the long lost youngster. We related the parable of the prodigal son. It did no good. The island squirrels didn't want him around. We tried to sneak peanuts to him and our attempt only added fuel to the fire of anger. Let him touch a single peanut and the chattering took on new fierceness. No-Mo did a great deal of chattering himself, but it was mostly flung back over his flying tail as he fled from his pursuers.

Hi-Bub worked himself into the midst of the contest. He was militantly on No-Mo's side. He talked until his tongue was worn out from lisping. He ran after No-Mo trying to give him food, but No-Mo merely thought he was one more persecutor, and only sped away the faster.

It was a wild time indeed. The habitual quiet of the Sanctuary was completely lost. The air was filled with the voices of the four squirrels, Hi-Bub's constant contribution and the cries of several blue jays who seemed happy just to find something to yell about. No-Mo was so upset that he could not eat even when we found an opportunity to place food before him. He kept right on scolding without taking a single bite, until one of the other three located him once more and the battle was on again.

Hi-Bub pleaded with the visiting squirrel to "thwim away." He promised him all the peanuts he could eat. But No-Mo had no notion of leaving the island. In fact, he had definite designs on More-Mo's cherished attic. While we sat at dinner, the excitement in this department developed. There had been a brief lull in hostilities. Apparently No-Mo had been lost sight of. From our dining-room window we saw No-Mo race across the ground bearing a pine cone. He went over the route we had seen him use a hundred times, up a little balsam tree, across the kitchen roof and through the hole that had been chewed into the attic. As soon as his feet touched the boards over our heads, a fierce scramble took place. We heard two squirrels screaming with rage. Out came No-Mo hotly pursued by the now frantic More-Mo. They established new speed records up and down trees, through bushes, across roofs and by long graceful jumps right through the air. Still-Mo and Two-Mo chattered constantly some little way off, as if saying, "Get him! Scalp him! Run him out of town!"

Hi-Bub's evening and night were all that he had anticipated. The three of us were out in the old canoe as the sun went down in crimson glory. We drifted along darkening shores as twilight cast its silence over the forest, though in the distance we could still hear the chickaree argument on our island. We worked our way up the winding course of a creek, saw a beaver, saw a deer, heard a loon cry and a fox bark. Bub was supposed to tell us when he was sleepy so we could take him to his waiting bed in the tent. He told us, but not in words. He was warmly wrapped in a kapoc jacket, seated on a cushion and leaning comfortably against a back rest. Presently he was having a terrible struggle with his eyelids, and with his head. These things simply wouldn't stay where he put them. His head was determined to fall against his back rest, and his eyelids were bound to close. He jerked them back in place a dozen times, but they wouldn't stay. He made the trip back to the island through dreamland. Giny and I paddled as softly as ever we did in stalking a deer. Hi-Bub claimed the right of childhood to sleep when sleep feels best.

When we approached the boathouse Bub awakened partially. We hoped he might not lose his sleepiness during the process of going to bed. But right there Hi-Bub exercised another prerogative of childhood. That is to stay awake when one feels like it. The squirrels were still chattering out in the darkness. He became much concerned as to No-Mo's welfare, and continued to worry in spite of our reassurances. Then came the barrage of questions. What would we do if a bear came? I assured him one would not come in all probability, and even if one did there was no danger. Bub wanted some danger. Wouldn't the bear even scratch the tent? No, the bear wouldn't scratch the tent. But what if one came inside and couldn't get out again? I affirmed that a bear wouldn't do that. He wondered if there were any Indians around. Of course, in a tent one would have to have Indians.

"The Indians all left this region many years ago, Bub," I told him, my own eyes getting heavy.

"Wouldn't there be just one left maybe?" he argued hopefully.

"No, Bub, there isn't even one."

"But couldn't there be one that—that no one know-th about?" Bub was determined to have his Indian.

Well, all right, I gave in. There could be one that no one knows about. Bub laughed delightedly.

"Do you know, Bub," I said earnestly, "the first question your father and mother will ask me when I take you home?"

"Huh?"

"They will want to know if you went to sleep the way you should, and I suppose they wouldn't want you to come back again unless you did. Don't you think we ought to be quiet now?"

"Uh-huh!"

The side of our tent house is arranged so panels in the side will slide down leaving a great screened opening. I had opened one of these panels to let into the tent the fresh air and still loveliness of the forest night. We were quiet now. Bub talked no more, though the red squirrels broke out with their dispute intermittently. After a few minutes I raised my head and cautiously peeked at Bub. The little rascal was no more asleep than Still-Mo. I could see his round little face on the pillow, his eyes looking out into the night reflecting the starlight, while his mind dealt with thoughts available only to childhood.

I lowered my head quietly. This was his right, this stealing of moments or even hours away from rest that they might be used for greater purposes. Still vivid in my memory were the camps I had known in childhood, down on the slow-flowing rivers of Illinois. I had stolen lingering glances at the stars when I was supposed to be asleep. I had looked with awe at the silhouettes of trees against the heavenly glow, listened to the mystery of cricket calls, felt marvelous things about creation that have been lost since in adult nonsense.

Go on, Bub, thought I, daydream away as much of the night as you wish. Life will give you few adventures that will match the miracle of your first night in a tent. The world you see is your world. Tonight you have no competitor. Drink that poetry you look upon right into your heart. It will nourish you in sterner days.

"Tham!" Bub's voice startled me, it was so unexpected.

"Yes, Bub."

"Are you afraid to go out in the dark?"

"Why no, Bub. Why do you ask?"

"I want a drink of water!"

That's an old trick too. It used to work for me, and now it worked for Hi-Bub.

XVI

A DREAM THAT WOULDN'T STAY PUT

THE blessed day and hour came when Sandy stood in our midst. Sergeant Sandy, seasoned soldier, proven hero, had returned to the Sanctuary. We marvel much at the unexplained migrations of birds and beasts. There is a sweet mystery about the ability of a bird to wing its way several thousand miles to the south in autumn, and then return over that distance the next spring to a certain nest in a chosen tree. It savors of divine guidance. But there is a grand intelligence at work in our lives too. If we were not so close to the details we would marvel even more at the power that had taken Sandy over lands and seas through a thousand dangers and now back to this tiny little spot on a great globe.

I looked at the boy in unrestrained admiration. His moves were those of a thoroughly trained and well-schooled athlete. There was an ease about him that spoke of a great reservoir of strength immediately at his call. I could not see that he had changed greatly. In fact, I believe the idea that war experiences cause great deterioration in youth, turn hair gray over night, and alter character, is much overstated. There is no doubt of the severity of their trials. Horror is part of the whole fallacy of war. But I have seen many young men and women who have waded through the most savage battles and yet were very much the same after the experience as before.

It was the same old Sandy who stood talking to us at the cabin the morning of his arrival. We were all standing, much too excited to sit down. Sandy's smile was fixed on his lips. His old natural modesty was obvious. Mention of his service, particularly his heroism, embarrassed him noticeably. Reluctantly he related some war experiences, but always sugar-coated with his sense of humor. Even the time when he was on the beaches of Salerno and shells were falling about thicker than hailstones, he laughed as he told how frightened he was and how he disappeared into the ground "faster than a woodchuck." His medal was nothing. It didn't cost him anything, so he took it. It was all because the fellows on the other side wanted some good chow that they surrendered. He didn't want to take them prisoners; they forced him to do it.

Yes, Sandy was the same old boy. Giny had gone into the kitchen to see about the all important matter of breakfast. She returned to ask Sandy how he would like his eggs cooked. Sandy saw her coming and winked at me.

"I saw a boid today," said he, in matter-of-fact way.

"Not a *boid,* Sandy," I corrected, catching my cue, "you mean *bird.*"

"No! No!" screamed Giny. "Not that, please!"

But Sandy persisted.

"Well, it choiped like a boid and it was after a woim!"

"Not a *woim,* Sandy, it was a *worm!*"

"But it squoimed like a woim, and it was inna doit!"

"Not *doit*—you mean *dirt!*"

"Well, it looked doity, and it choimed like a squoip!"

The last sentence was finished on the fly. Giny had been holding her head in agony, and as this crowning bit of foolishness came out, she grasped a mop and imitated the charge of the light brigade. Sandy and I retreated in disorder. We went out the front door at full speed, followed closely by the mop. Sandy didn't stop until he was halfway up a tall tree.

No question about it now—Sandy hadn't changed a bit!

By the time breakfast was finished, Sandy had heard much about Hi-Bub. He was ready and anxious to meet the young naturalist. He had been told also the rather discouraging facts about Buddie the old canoe.

"You think Buddie will never go on the search for Sanctuary Lake then?" he asked.

"It looks that way," I replied. "Of course there are other canoes."

Sandy shook his head. "Buddie belongs to that expedition—if and when!" he insisted. "Half of the dream would be lacking without Buddie."

We went down to look the old craft over. Sandy stood back while I drew away the canvas covering, and when he saw the canoe his eyes mellowed with affection.

"Buddie, old pal, I guess you're wearing too many service stripes." Sandy examined the craft with critical eye. "You ought to have the Purple Heart and Congressional Medal of Honor for that one," he said, patting the copper plate in the canoe bow. "And every one of those scars you got doing something for someone."

He turned the canoe over carefully. "Believe I can strengthen that," he said, indicating a broken brace. "I brought a new kind of glue that will fill those cracks too. Mind if I work on it a bit?"

"It's all yours, Sandy," I laughed. "Whatever you do for Buddie you are doing for us, too."

"I'll be working at it," declared our soldier.

Now from the mainland I heard a familiar voice.

"What in the world is that?" asked Sandy.

I cautioned him to silence, and pointed to the nearest point on shore. "Peanut-th!" came the call. "Th-tubby, Noothanth, I got peanut-th!"

"Hi-Bub?" asked Sandy.

"Hi-Bub!" I affirmed.

Before I went over to get the boy, I coached Sandy on his behavior. He simply must not let Hi-Bub down. "If he wants you to lift that canoe with one hand, you lift it," I insisted. "If he wants you to jump up on the boathouse, you jump!" Sandy pleaded inability, but I replied that was no excuse. He must live up to the boy's expectations.

I asked Sandy to be standing in silence near the canoe when I returned. It was sort of a mean trick. Hi-Bub had not been told the exact day on which our soldier would arrive. Therefore he was expecting no other adventure than putting in a few hours with the island animals. I brought him over in a boat, and landed him without his suspecting anything unusual.

"Hi-Bub," I said as he stood on the boathouse pier.

"Yeth?" he answered, probably expecting to hear some new stunt by the red squirrels.

"Look at the old canoe."

Hi-Bub did. There stood Sandy, a perfect picture of military attention. Bub made a little choking sound in his throat. He stopped dead in his tracks.

"This is Sandy, Hi-Bub."

Hi-Bub's eyes passed the dinner-plate size this time. His characteristic little "Oh-h-h-h" was hardly audible. His arms hung limply at his sides, and his mouth stood open. When Sandy started to walk toward him, Bub looked as if he wanted to run but couldn't.

"Hello there, big boy," Sandy was saying as he neared the entranced child. "I've been hearing a lot about you. Something tells me you and I are going to be pals. How about shaking hands?"

"Oh-h-h-h," said Hi-Bub, staring at the soldier without a wink. He laid his hand, thumb and all, into that of the sergeant and let Sandy do all the shaking.

"I picked up a compass over in Italy, and brought it back for just such a boy as you," Sandy said, trying to talk a way through the inertia that gripped Bub. "Suppose you and I go up to my bag and get it. Want to?"

Hi-Bub was starting to regain consciousness. "A computh?" he said.

"Yes, a computh," Sandy lisped. "Come on, maybe you will show me some of these animals too. What do you say?"

The two grand American boys headed up the little hill

hand in hand. It was a symbolic picture. So it must ever be in the land of free men if our race is to grow in character and right living. The stronger and older must take the younger and inexperienced by the hand, gently but wisely to guide him. And the younger must look to the strength and wisdom of the older that these qualities may grow in him.

Someone capable at shorthand should have been around to take down Hi-Bub's dissertation on nature that day. Sandy certainly heard a lot of things he had never heard before. The soldier had to meet each animal individually—Link Sausage, Bratwurst, Salami, Wiener, Thuringer, Patty and O. Bologna. He was told the special characteristics of each creature. He heard of the super-intelligence of Still-Mo, and the particular traits of More-Mo, Two-Mo and No-Mo. The story of Racket was related, now a very happy tale, for the young raccoon was doing wonderfully. Fragments of this boy-soldier conversation reached us occasionally. We heard them practicing at that dizzy squoip dialogue. Bub didn't get it exactly right, but near enough to make his parents wonder to the point of asking me some days hence what were "boids, woims, squoips, etc."

Sandy and I took Bub home in the canoe later that day, while Giny prepared dinner. The soldier was a little awkward with his paddle at first, but soon regained his old rhythm. Hi-Bub watched him with unabated admiration.

"Thandy make-th it go thum, huh?" he commented. I mentioned that I was paddling too, and might have a little credit coming for our speed, but this made no difference to Hi-Bub. Sandy was all that mattered.

"Good-by, Hi-Bub, you bum!" said Sandy, as we landed the youngster on his pier.

"Good-by Thandy—you Thquoip!" laughed Hi-Bub.

"Come over again," we called in unison, as we backed away.

"I thure will," said Hi-Bub.

And he sure did. As long as Sandy was there, Bub was as regular as the sunrise, and only a couple hours later. I don't know which one was more smitten with the other, however. If Hi-Bub was very late after the unappointed but expected hour, Sandy commenced to worry about him. The soldier understood the little fellow very well from the start.

"Do some folks exaggerate things a little bit sometimes?" he asked me at the close of that first day.

"Well, it does happen, and not a little bit either," I commented.

"Then Hi-Bub has never been to Africa? or Italy? or England?—all the places I have been?"

"No, and he was never in the jungle playing with wildcats either."

"Oh-oh, I get it," said Sandy with a laugh.

Evening at the Sanctuary was quiet, misty, drowsy. It was warm, but we built a modest gratefire just for its light. We sat before it letting conversation fall where it might, like the proverbial chips. In the news of the world had been some thought-staggering announcements. A new power had been liberated, exceeding anything heretofore known to science. Explosives had in a few minutes of time wiped out two large enemy cities. Sandy refrained from much comment. He had seen cities that had undergone bombardment. Reports said that the destruction by the latest bombs was far more devastating than what he had looked upon. It seemed incredible, even sickening to him. "I suppose it must be done," he said soberly. "It may even be most merciful and actually save lives. But it is sad that people cannot learn right living without such terrible lessons."

The world press was full of guesses. Some thought the war in Asia was near its end, some were convinced it was not.

Sandy arose and walked to the window. A belated moon was rising over the pine trees along the eastern shore of our lake. It laid a path of shimmering gold through the waters.

"Know something?" asked Sandy.

"Not much—what are you thinking?" I replied.

"That same moon is shining on Sanctuary Lake. The moon knows where it is even if we don't. Just think, somewhere away off in that wilderness that place is waiting for us. Right now there are moose walking along its shores, wild geese nesting, and ducks, and loons—and we aren't there!"

Giny and I groaned in sympathy.

"Where's a map of Canada?" asked Sandy. "Got one? Let's get it out and whip up some enthusiasm."

We found one and the enthusiasm followed. We spread the map out before the fire, the flames giving us an uneven lighting. We might have turned on a real light, but a map of canoe country never shows up as well in any other illumination as by firelight. We lay upon the floor, picking out loved spots in that canoe country. Our fingers and pencils bumped into each other as we traced routes we had taken.

"There is Yum-Yum Lake," exclaimed Sandy. "Remember the camp we had on the flat rock right near that portage into Kahshahpiwi?"

"Yes, and I remember that portage too, the toughest in the Quetico," I commented.

"Here is that little bass lake near Lac La Croix. It had no name, but it was opposite our camp on this island. Do you remember it?"

Did I remember it? It was filled with fish, and while we have never made anyone believe the story, we actually caught bass without a hook. We tied pieces of red flannel on the line, and cast with a fly rod from shore. The bass struck so savagely and held so determinedly we could lift them to shore.

"I never got anyone to believe that either," said Sandy. "The fellows in the army just laugh and say, 'OK, Paul Bunyan, how about your blue ox?'"

We reviewed campsites for a few minutes, then began

to speculate on where Sanctuary Lake might be. Maybe it would be one of those unnamed ponds west of Sarah Lake, maybe in that cluster north of Sioux Lookout, maybe east of Northern Light Lake, maybe north of the Maligne River.

Sandy the Squoip had now shed all semblance of military dignity. He was the carefree boy again. He rolled on his back on the floor, and looked up dreamily.

"Aw, gee, can't we go?" he said. "We could leave in the morning and be out in that woods by night."

"It would be grand!" said Giny.

"Marvelous!" said I.

"Oh-h-h-h-h," said Sandy, somewhat after the pattern of Hi-Bub.

"Buddie probably couldn't stand it," I reminded the other two.

"And we haven't any gasoline," agreed Giny.

"And no tires," said I.

"Oh-h-h-h-h!" groaned Sandy.

XVII

CARROTS AND COMICS

OUR woodchuck family was quite well grown by the time Sandy arrived. We had to look carefully to distinguish the young ones from Link Sausage, the mother. Their youthful prankishness was already fading and they were taking life more seriously. Each retained those individual characteristics which identified it, however. Thuringer was more quiet and aloof. He was generally found alone, depending little on his mother for food or direction. While they made common use of certain of their underground homes, on sort of an old homestead idea, Thuringer in particular kept digging at his own cave dwelling far back in the brush. Bratwurst was saucy but improving in disposition, Salami nervous and forever on the move, Wiener increasingly shy and in fact seldom seen, while Patty declined to grow up and remained somewhat tied to his mother's apron strings. O. Bologna gained in stature and assumed importance. In size he looked not a pound lighter than his mother.

Sandy had a lesson in woodchuck-ology the second morning he was at the Sanctuary. He was treated to the rare sight of seeing the six youngsters all at once, sitting in a huddle, eating bread that Giny had contributed to them. They were all upright, facing various directions, each with a bit of the food held in its front feet while chewing went on at a mile-a-minute pace. "Looks like one of our old chow lines," commented Sandy. "Only our GI's can eat faster than that."

Wiener was pointed out as he dashed away several times, frightened at no one knows what. Thuringer sat sedately at one side, chewing less hurriedly than the rest, but certainly getting his share. Patty, looking worried and abused, sat beside big blustery O. Bologna. He always chose to be near the big smart alec, and it is hard to know just why. He always got in trouble there. It wasn't long until it happened again. O. Bologna finished his piece of bread before Patty had got well started into his. There was plenty more on the ground—but no, O. Bologna had to hit Patty with his front paws, bite him on the back of the neck and, while the little punching bag ran squealing away, the big bully picked up the bread he had dropped and resumed his chewing. Typically Patty came whimpering back, picked up another piece of bread and sat down squarely beside O. Bologna to eat it.

O. Bologna's real disposition was revealed to Sandy a few minutes later. The bread had been consumed to the last crust. The woodchucks were not satisfied and went nosing about picking up the crumbs. Giny then contributed a handful of cabbage leaves. There was a wild scramble as she opened the door. Six woodchucks disappeared into the ground in no time flat. Sandy roared. "Just like our outfit when a dive bomber showed up," he said.

The ground hogs were not gone long, however. Little brown noses were poking out of holes in the ground, looking around to see how serious the situation was. And there, within sight and scent, was a pile of cabbage leaves! Several of them came and began tasting the next course of their dinner. It was much to their liking. Four of them had arrived and stood with noses to the center of a little huddle, chewing away at the cabbage, when up strutted O. Bologna. He rose high on his hind legs to see what it was that so attracted his brothers and sister. Giving a scream, he dashed right into the middle of the huddle, sending the other chucks scampering wildly in four directions. Thereupon he picked up one cabbage leaf and sat down upon the others, and indulged a solo banquet. Several chucks came close but not one got up to the food again. "Nazi!" yelled Sandy at him, but O. Bologna didn't mind what he was called, just so long as he kept possession of the cabbage—which proves that Sandy was right.

Our soldier had some plans that day, but delayed with them until Hi-Bub showed up. While waiting for the inevitable call of "peanut-th" Sandy worked at the old canoe. I heard him singing and whistling as he worked. The very touch of the craft delighted him. Several times I caught him standing back a few feet admiring it. "Beautiful lines! Beautiful lines!" he said. "Just see that graceful upturn at the bow and stern, and that breadth of beam. And the old boy rests on the water as lightly as a milkweed seed."

Once he came walking past the cabin windows with the canoe on his shoulders, portage style. He wasn't going anywhere in particular, just wanted the feeling of carrying it around. "I'm going to fix up that brace, if you don't mind," he called to me. "Buddie groans a little when I lift him, but I believe he can take a lot of abuse yet."

"OK, Sandy you Squoip," I answered. "Do whatever you want to, but don't get any dreams we can't carry out."

When Hi-Bub arrived, rosy-cheeked and short of breath from a hurried trip across the trail, Sandy stopped his work on the canoe and took up his job with the boy.

"Got an idea," he said to the interested Hi-Bub. "We're going to have some fun with that smart alec old O. Bologna." Sandy told in detail the woodchuck episode of the morning. "We'll give that fellow something to think about, and see if he won't be a little kinder to Patty and the others in the future."

"We thure will!" agreed Hi-Bub, bristling with importance.

The two of them took a good-sized carrot, tied it on a string, and hung it near the hole where O. Bologna was most often seen. Then they moved back some distance and waited to see what would happen. There was an uneventful interval, which gave Hi-Bub a chance to lisp out a yarn about some strange creature he had seen on the trail while coming over. It seems that Bub didn't get a real good look at the animal, so according to his own admission he might be wrong, but it looked as if it had a horn in its nose. What color was it? Why, it wasn't any color—it was big! How big? Bub looked around for something to measure it by.

"Was it as big as a dog?" asked Sandy, trying to be helpful.

"Oh-h-h-h, bigger'n 'at!"

"Maybe as big as two dogs," suggested the soldier.

"Yeth," agreed Bub.

"Did it have front feet?" asked Sandy, getting more excited.

"Yeth!" Bub was getting stirred up by his story too.

"And hind feet?"

"Yeth!"

"Did it have two eyes, or three?"

"Two!"

"And did it make a noise like this?" Sandy sniffed violently.

"Yeth!" Bub was agreeing to everything now.

"Did it run sort of like a fish?"

"Yeth!"

"Oh-oh! Hi-Bub, you have seen a Whooperdoo!" said Sandy seriously. "Yessir, that was a Whooperdoo, sure as you're born."

"It wuth?" Hi-Bub should never have started such a thing with a GI. After dealing with the endless rumors that circulate in military service, a soldier is a past master at imagination.

"It sure was!" affirmed Sandy. "Strange thing about them, the young ones are larger than the parents. Bet this

146 *A TIPPY CANOE AND CANADA TOO*

one you saw was only a few days old. Next year he will grow so small you can hardly find him. He eats bubble berries, but never swallows the seeds. . . ."

I don't know where this story would have led if O. Bologna hadn't peeked out of the ground near the hanging carrot that minute. I sighed with relief. Sandy looked relieved too. It is hard to get such a yarn stopped once it is well started.

O. Bologna was giving us all plenty to think about. He spied the carrot, which was about his own length from the ground and swinging slightly in the breeze. He regarded the odd thing intently, an expression of amazement creeping over his face. Had it been on the ground, where any self-respecting carrot is supposed to be, he would have pounced upon it at once. But this was up in the air where only leaves should grow. Cautiously he advanced toward it, as if any step might spring a trap. The wind blew a bit harder, the carrot gyrated on the string—and O. Bologna made a crash dive for his fox hole! Sandy laughed loud, slapping his knee with the hollow of his hand. Bub slapped his too. Whatever Sandy did must be right!

Almost immediately O. Bologna stuck his head out again. Could he really have seen what he thought he saw? Was there such a thing as a carrot that hangs up in the air and makes a pass at a fellow when he goes near it? Yes, there it hung, and it was just a few inches from his nose!

Now a woodchuck has a marvelous ability to outwait and outstare almost anything. Many times when I have been trying to make pictures of these little Sausages, I have seen them enter statuelike poses and hold them for many minutes without batting an eye, until I have deserted my purpose and given up with the promise to catch them some other time. O. Bologna called forth this woodchuck talent to serve him in the carrot problem now looking him in the face. He fixed his eyes on the puzzling thing. His whole body became as inert as if it had been frozen. There wasn't the twitch of a muscle or the bat of an eye. He reminded me of the rigid pointing of a bird dog. He stayed at least a quarter of an hour in that position. We laughed at him, and called to him, but he would not move. Perhaps he would have spent the rest of the summer that way, if a blessed breeze hadn't come along and set the carrot to dancing. O. Bologna vanished. The move was almost too quick for the eye. Hi-Bub described it pretty well.

Giny heard us laughing and called out asking if O. Bologna had run away.

"No!" said Hi-Bub, giggling, "he didn't run, he's just gone."

That was it, the animal didn't seem to run at all. One moment he was there and the next he wasn't.

O. Bologna apparently decided the carrot conundrum was too great for him. Presently he ran past it directly over to the back steps of the cabin. There his mother emerged to meet him. Hi-Bub and Sandy insisted he had gone to tell her about it, and certainly it looked that way. He ran his nose up near her ear as if whispering. When they were side by side the difference in their sizes and expressions was obvious. O. Bologna was still a youngster, his mother still his guardian. Link Sausage looked over toward the curious carrot. She licked her chops as she thought how it would taste. Sandy told Bub her comments probably went something like this: "Don't you worry about that thing, son. I never saw a carrot in my life I couldn't handle. It does look sorta funny sailing round in the air like a butterfly. But I'll teach it a thing or two about scaring my child. Just stand back and watch your maw!"

Well, "Maw" had a harder job before her than she fancied. We had more laughs than we anticipated, too. I felt concerned about Hi-Bub, he got to giggling so. He climbed up in Sandy's lap so he could see better, which was a good excuse anyway.

Link Sausage showed no timidity about the crazy carrot. She walked over to it, reaching up with her front feet. The wind was blowing moderately and carried it away. She jumped after it, giving it a push. It got to swinging wildly, finally making a circular motion with Link following, making frantic efforts to catch it, but instead giving it little shoves that made it travel the faster. The wind gave it nudges too. Link became bewildered. It was more than she had bargained for. The carrot was circling her now in a great arc, while she turned round and round trying to keep track of it. The aggravating thing was always behind her. For just a moment she caught hold of it with her front feet and sank her sharp teeth into it. She started to back away. The stubborn carrot would not come along. She tugged and tugged, but the string wouldn't yield. In the meantime, her problem became complicated. O. Bologna came up close, thinking the carrot would soon be down, hors de combat. Patty appeared from somewhere and prepared to chisel in on the spoils. The two of them got right in Link's way. Patty bumped into O. Bologna, and that started a fight. Link made a pass at her troublesome offspring and lost her grip on the carrot, which promptly started on its circuitous route again. Now she *was* mad. She made a run at O. Bologna, chasing him squealing into the ground. Then she gave Patty the same treatment. With these troublesome "brats" out of the way, she returned to the carrot now angry enough to pulverize it. The swinging had slowed down somewhat, and she caught the tantalizing vegetable quickly. Ordinarily she would have sat calmly nibbling at such a delectable bit of food, but not now. Giving a little squeak of temper she bit the big carrot squarely in two; half of it remained in the string, the other half rolled down the hill, Link racing after it.

Patty reappeared on the scene. Link was gone, and O. Bologna still in the subterranean depths. The stage was all Patty's and he put on an act that made us reach within ourselves to bring out the last laughs we had left. Patty, runt that he was, got right under the carrot and standing on tiptoes did his level best to reach it. He was just about two inches short. He stretched and reached with all his might, but he couldn't quite make it. I never saw anything else look so funny, so awkward and so wholly pathetic as that little fellow did. He would tire of his stretching, and sit on his haunches to rest, but his eyes never left that carrot. Then he would try all over again, his loose hide drooping down in a comical way. Hi-Bub described the appearance very well when he said, "He lookth like hith panth ith comin' off."

Giny couldn't stand to have Patty teased any further. She brought out a big, long carrot as a consolation prize.

O. Bologna had returned, and when the new carrot was tossed to the ground, he began chewing at one end while Patty chewed at the other. The carrot was long enough to keep them separated for a few minutes—though no longer.

Sandy finally got over his laughing enough to say, "When you can have that much fun in this world with just a carrot and a string and a woodchuck, how can nations ever find time to waste in starting a war?"

It is a very good question at that!

XVIII

WHEN SOUL SINGS

IT WAS August 14, 1945. The date made no difference to our island animals. The red squirrels hustled about as usual, and the woodchucks' social difficulties continued. Racket, the 'coon, plied about in full sight. His coat was growing more beautiful and his step more steady. Ratzy-Watzy endured some expert taunting by More-Mo. A mother robin led several teasing youngsters about on the ground, giving them instruction in the art of locating, extricating and gobbling down selected worms. But with Sandy, Giny and myself there was seething, pulsing excitement that kept us disquieted.

Through the still day we watched and listened into the distance. We had difficulty getting interested in anything. We were waiting, our fears constantly in clash with our hopes. Hi-Bub did not come over. He was kept home by his parents—waiting, waiting for the same anxious reason we were. The terms for concluding the war in the Pacific lay before the nations. While statesmen pondered, the world listened breathlessly. Every heart had a tangible interest in what was to happen.

We have never permitted a radio at the Sanctuary through the years. This was the only day we regretted that policy. We had a high stake in the news. Already several boys near and dear to us were fighting in those far-off islands. Sandy, the grand lad who now gave us happiness through his presence at our cabin, would have to help win that war if it went on. We could feel the strain the world lived under, and we wanted news as soon as news was available.

The best we could do was arrange for someone, a close friend who lived a few miles away, to come and tell us. He was one of tremendous vocal power. His great "war whoop" had echoed on our shores before. On a still day or night it could be heard for several miles. When the news came, if it were favorable, he was to come down the lakes in his own canoe, "yelling his head off." If it were unfavorable, he was to come in silence, and we would gather in a circle and steel ourselves for more of the unwonted struggle of war.

It was one of those afternoons that get caught on a hook and seem never to move an inch. The sun had passed the zenith and we hoped it would move faster on the downhill side, but it did not. One o'clock, two o'clock, three o'clock—each hour came and settled down as if it meant to stay forever. Sandy worked at further repairs on Buddie. Giny baked a layer cake to celebrate in case the news was good, to console us if it were not. I milled about in my papers and made some futile attempts at writing. But our attention was focused down the lakes, in the direction from which news would come.

Some way or other the day reached six P.M. At the pace it had traveled it was a wonder it ever got there. The sun was near the horizon, and for a while looked as if it didn't intend to go any farther. Still there was no news. Could our friend have forgotten the arrangements? Not likely—he is not the kind to forget. The news had not been announced yet, or he would be coming. We ate dinner, a delicious one, but our appreciation was lacking.

As dusk settled softly on the forest, we walked down to our campfire site and started a little blaze. We could hear distant sounds better here than in the cabin. We listened so intently the very silence seemed to roar. Our judgment of sounds was distorted.

"There! There he comes now," exclaimed Giny as she detected a voice far off in the night. We listened anxiously. It came again and was the call of the barred owl. We laughed a little, joked a little, but there was no need to conceal the tension we were under.

Sandy was the least affected. He hid his hopes behind a conviction that the war could not end this way. But his conversation was spotted with remarks about friends who were in that theater of operations, and gratitude for their safety if the fighting stopped.

So many creatures called that night, it seemed they were deliberately taunting us. Two porcupines indulged an argument, and their voices dominated the silence for a few moments. A heron was feeding back in a dark bay, and occasionally gave its harsh cry. Coyotes staged a convention back in the forest, all talking at once. A raccoon trilled, and a woodchuck whistled.

Then in a moment when our attention had wavered

came the sound for which we were listening. Far, far down the lakes we heard a strong and distant "Wahoo." We were on our feet instantly.

"No doubt about that voice!" said Giny excitedly. "He's coming, and he's coming ayelling!"

Sandy and I combined our efforts and sent a powerful shout out into the darkness. "Wahoo," came the answer, now a little closer. The word is not in the dictionary, and it never will be, but that night it had greater meaning to us than the most chosen language. It meant defeat of aggression and surrender of aggressors. It meant the saving of thousands and thousands of our boys. It meant the return to normalcy in living, the chance to think, work and plan in line with natural human ideals. It meant the lifting of the burden of worry from the minds of those who wait for the return of loved ones.

Our messenger came on and landed, his voice tired but his ardor undimmed. It was as our signal indicated. Japan had surrendered! We threw our arms around each other and danced for joy.

"Let's have something to eat and lots of it!" I exclaimed. "I paid no attention to my dinner, now I'm hungry."

"Food! Let there be food!" agreed our messenger.

"We want chow! We want chow!" Sandy had begun a chant in which we all joined.

Giny was not to be carried away on this enthusiasm. The moment had too deep a significance to her.

"All right," she said, "you shall have your food. But there is something more important. We have some gratitude to express. Will you join me?"

We did join her. Out in the starlight, with our campfire sending shadows dancing up the trunks of trees, and all nature bowing head with us we said in unison:

> Our Father which art in heaven,
> Hallowed be Thy name.
> Thy Kingdom come.
> Thy will be done in earth, as it is in heaven.
> Give us this day our daily bread;
> And forgive us our debts, as we forgive our debtors.
> And lead us not into temptation, but deliver us from evil;
> For Thine is the kingdom, and the power, and the glory, forever.
> Amen.

XIX

A DREAM COMES TRUE

I AM often led to speculate on the evidence of divine design there is even in the small events of our lives. My convictions in the matter are stronger than my ability to express them. There are, of course, false desires in which "Ye ask, and receive not, because ye ask amiss, that ye may consume it upon your lusts." But when we keep our hearts clean, living to the best of our ability the way we know beyond cavil to be right, there is a certain element of prophecy in our desires, from the least to the greatest of them. In the unfolding of spiritual character, which is the great goal of all life's experiences, destiny often makes use of things which human judgment may deem relatively unimportant.

The yearning we had to go in search of our little Sanctuary Lake was of this nature. The desire wouldn't be kept down. We had pushed it aside, presumably dismissing it because of wartime conditions, gas rations, and the fact that our old canoe looked unfit for the trip. But the idea simply would not take *no* for an answer and kept teasing at us like a pampered child.

For the first several days after peace news, we were occupied in an effort to comprehend what it meant. The change was almost as startling and sudden as if guns had been shooting right there at the Sanctuary, and now had ceased. Little did we realize how this war had woven itself into our lives, influencing everything we did, thought and said. The change to peaceful ways of living felt strange and highly challenging.

"Guess I'll be selling shoestrings sooner than I thought I would," said Sandy with a laugh, but one could feel that it wasn't all happiness back in his thought. A little of the old self-doubt and feeling of being a misfit was in evidence.

Few will ever forget the way events stampeded forth those momentous hours, each stepping on the heels of the one preceding it. Troop movements were altered, some halted. Demobilization plans were announced, and immediately begun. War contracts were canceled at a bewildering rate.

Most startling to civilian habits came the announcement that gas rationing was ended. It was hard to understand the new liberty. We sat at luncheon one noon talking over the situation, and I held in my hand a sheet of gas coupons. "How values change!" I was remarking. "A week ago these things were more valuable to me than gold notes. Now they aren't even good wastepaper!"

"They might serve a purpose at that, if you save them." Sandy was thinking of civilian life. "Some day a year from now when you think you have problems, take a look at them and they will remind you of times that were worse."

Giny had the clearer, more unselfish view, as Giny always does. "It is so good that people can go places now," she was saying. "Everyone is tired and needing the refreshment of nature. There can be trips into the country again, fishing trips, camping trips...."

She got no farther. Sandy jumped to his feet, highly excited. "Did you hear what she said?" he demanded of me. "She said *people could go places;* she said *camping trips!* How about it?"

"How about what?" I asked, as if I didn't know.

"Why, going in search of Sanctuary Lake! We have the gas now. We have the time. We have the ambition. What are we waiting for?" Sandy was gesticulating like a political orator.

"But what about Buddie? I doubt if the old canoe can stand the trip," I argued against my own inclinations.

"I fixed the brace," said Sandy, and he knew he was winning. "We'll take lots of patching material along and make the trip on glue and varnish if we have to. It will just add pep to the adventure."

"But our tires," Giny said weakly. "Could we trust them?"

"They aren't really so bad." I came to the defense now. "We can carry patches for them too!"

"But the animals," persisted Giny. "They would leave the island if we did not help them out with food."

"I can get someone to come and feed them," I continued.

We stood looking at each other in a state of suspended animation for a moment, unable to realize our freedom.

We *could* go! The trip would have a little risk to it, a little extra challenge—but we *could* go. I looked at Giny and nodded a little "Yes." She looked at Sandy, and did the same. Sandy nodded at me. In a moment our heads were bobbing up and down like those agreeable Santa Claus toys that adorn Christmas counters.

"How soon?" asked Sandy.

"Tomorrow morning at dawn!" said I.

"Oh, we can't!" said Giny.

"But we can!" I insisted.

"Wa-ho-o-o-o!" yelled Sandy. "Let's go! We leave for Sanctuary Lake at dawn. Get the lead out of your shoes! Let's get going!"

And we "got going!" Have you ever chopped into a half-decayed log, penetrated unwittingly into a nest of ants and noted the explosion of energy and activity that results? Every insect races about to go somewhere and do something in the quickest way possible. The result is the wildest confusion. That was the way things went at the Sanctuary. I don't know just how it could be done, but Sandy said each of us started in three directions at once. Our soldier was assigned to a final checkup on the canoe, paddles, yoke, and the assembling of the all-important repair kit. Giny took from old letter files lists of the supplies we had taken on previous trips into the canoe country. It was well that we had such a list, for in the excitement we would have forgotten many important items. But here was a record of how much of each item we would need, so much per day per person.

My task in this melee of preparation was a pleasant one. I must get out the equipment—tents, packsacks, sleeping bags, ax, fishing tackle, cooking and eating utensils. There were two tents: one seven by nine foot made of oiled silk for Giny and me, and the other a one-man size for Sandy, looking like a large canvas envelope. The Squoip learned to love his little cloth cabin and affectionately called it his "portable tunnel."

A true camper is sentimental about his equipment. Articles that have known service in forest adventure take on a value that cannot be explained in usual commercial ratings. I lifted my old Duluth packsack, tested the strength of its buckles and straps. No lady of fashion ever felt more adoration for a priceless fur coat than did I for that stained, weathered, wrinkled old canvas sack. Across my mind flashed memory of the far-off places we had been together. There was my short-handled ax, in it some nicks from the rocks in the granite hills of the canoe country. Next I picked up our black, misshapen frying pan, with the folding handle. That precious old skillet! It had been in our service longer than even Buddie the canoe. I fondled it, thinking of the toothsome miracles it had produced of flapjacks, fried fish, and bacon in hidden, silent campsites of the far north. Even now, it was destined to produce more!

Within an hour the island had taken on the look of a rummage sale. There were little stacks of equipment everywhere. Sleeping bags were opened and spread in the sunshine for airing. Clothing for the trip was hung out on lines. Cameras, binoculars, compasses, maps, etc., made separate little piles, the sum total of which was confusing to say the least. Music was in the air. Giny sang as she worked at what seemed to be an impossible task. Sandy whistled constantly while he groomed the canoe, paddles and yoke. The canoe song, with its stirring swing, was the favorite. Alternately I joined one or the other—whomever I happened to be nearest.

Then came a damper on our enthusiasm. It was a little damper, but it toned us down nevertheless.

"Peanut-th!" came a faint voice in the distance, escaping our attention for a while because of our activity. "Peanut-th—Th-tubby, Noothanth, I got peanut-th!"

Sandy brought Hi-Bub over to the topsy-turvy island. The boy looked at the preparations with unconcealed dismay.

"We are going to Canada, Hi-Bub," I said in answer to the question written in his attitude. "We are leaving at dawn for a canoe trip."

"A canoe trip?" he repeated, his lips hardly moving.

"Yes, a canoe trip. We will be gone about a month. Won't that be fun?"

Bub didn't answer at first. He just stood staring at us, a question in his eyes.

"I never wuth on a canoe trip," he said soberly in the same tones used when he announced he had never been in a tent—and for the same promotional purpose.

"You will be—someday, Hi-Bub," I added with an

attempt at light-heartedness, "when you grow a little stronger, and those shoulders are a little broader. We'll take you up there."

"I'm thorta thtrong now," persisted Hi-Bub, but his hope was not high and his lip trembled. I knew not what to say, and a difficult silence resulted. Sandy came up to us, took in the situation but didn't know what to say either. We hadn't realized that our joy was somewhat at the expense of our lisping young friend. His visits to the island had become his life and his world. Now his happiness was falling in ashes about him. No use to minimize the hurt. To his little heart this was about the worst thing that could happen right then.

"But, Hi-Bub," I was saying, feeling that my words were futile, "we can't take you. We are going way back in the wilderness, farther than the jungle. We have to carry loads that you can't lift. Why, the canoe might even tip over. . . ."

"I can thwim," whispered Hi-Bub, his voice almost gone.

"Yes, I know, but your mother and daddy wouldn't let you go. You will grow up fast now, and it won't be long before we can take you."

"Sure!" said Sandy in his best he-man, hero-soldier voice. "Sure, Hi-Bub will be all right!"

The sergeant knelt down beside the boy. "You aren't going to cry. You are going to be a man!"

Hi-Bub didn't want to be a man that minute. He wanted to be a nine-year-old boy. He broke away from Sandy's arms and avoided mine. For a moment he looked around pathetically. He was so alone in the world. His lips quivered and a big tear coursed down his cheek. Then he discovered Giny, who was just coming out of the cabin to see what was going on. With a little gasp he ran and threw himself in her arms, and gave way to tears without reserve. This again is the right of childhood, to wash away its pains in its own tears in the understanding embrace of motherhood. Sandy and I looked at the two before us, feeling ourselves to be helpless, awkward brutes. This called for greater skill than any we possessed. The way Giny held our young pal, smoothed back his hair, and whispered just the right words in his ear was the sacred talent which no man can imitate.

For a moment we exchanged whispers. Could we take the little fellow? Surely his happy face and boyish enthusiasm would add much to any camp. There would not be room in one canoe, but we could rent another. However, the idea was unwise. This was not an adventure suited to his years. His parents would know that, and whatever we decided, their wisdom would never permit him to go. So we dismissed the thought. Besides, Giny had found something that was really halting the flow of tears.

"Do you know what we want you to do?" she asked, in a manner that foretold a very important announcement.

Hi-Bub didn't.

"We want you to come here and feed the squirrels, the woodchucks, and little Racket. Your daddy could bring you down fishing once in a while, and you could feed our pets. They are going to be lonesome and hungry. Would you do that?"

So an agreement was reached that Hi-Bub was to be custodian of the Sanctuary during our absence. The idea dried up tears, but it didn't entirely lift the gloom of his disappointment. He still watched our packing with longing in his big wide eyes, and once in a while I heard a little sniff as some stubborn tear refused to be kept back.

We showed Hi-Bub where we kept reserve food for the animals. There was a good supply of those invaluable fox biscuits, a concentrated product containing about everything needed in the diet of our creatures. There were peanuts galore, so all he had to do was land on the island and put out prescribed quantities of these supplies. It would be fun, at that, when this first hurt was healed by time, to feel the importance of being responsible for these animals.

Hi-Bub was taken home in a final ride in Buddie. Sandy and I escorted him, and Giny bade him good-by as we left. He was silent during the journey. At his pier we talked with his parents and they approved of the arrangements we had made. His daddy would bring him back every day or so.

Then we said good-by and began paddling away. Sandy and I wished we might be nine for just a few moments. The tug at our heart strings was strong, and we wished we didn't have to be men and hold back tears. We could have taken some mothering ourselves right then. Hi-Bub wasn't just an impetuous youngster teasing to do something he had no right to do. He loved the forest, and his little heart honestly yearned for adventure. We looked back and waved as he stood watching after us. We called to him, but there was no answer. His voice was gone again. When we were almost out of sight we saw his daddy pick him up and carry him toward their cabin. I fear there was another tear session for a mother to heal.

"I hadn't realized how that tiny fellow had got under my skin," said Sandy breaking the silence in which we had been paddling. "I almost wish we were not going."

But childhood has another quality which we really should never surrender. It clings to no yesterdays. This is additional evidence why we must be as little children before we can enter the kingdom of heaven. It was enough for Hi-Bub that he had known a day of heaviness. It could not mar the joy of the many interesting tomorrows which were coming. He arose to the occasion. The island animals never had such thorough attention before. Every need was met, with something extra thrown in. His work was the most important thing at his home. Daddy co-operated, and insisted that he had as good a time doing it as did Hi-Bub—but I suspect that he was often inconvenienced. Anyway, Hi-Bub grew his smile again, and his laugh that begins with a *whe-e-e-e* and ends with a *hick* was heard almost daily on our island.

XX

THRESHOLD OF THE WILDERNESS

GINY, Sandy and I stood looking out over the island-dotted vastness of Basswood Lake. Behind us lay a long trail which we had covered at good speed. With Buddie strapped on a canoe carrier atop our car, we had driven from our home over miles of pine-fringed roads to Ely, Minnesota. From there we had gone on a few miles farther to the little border town of Winton, populated mostly by Finnish lumberjacks. This was the end of the road in a northerly direction. Beyond was the land designed for canoe travel. A few hours were spent about the two towns while we gathered in the last of our supplies, and talked with Indians, guides and old-timers, seeking any information that might lead us toward the wilderness lake of which we dreamed. There were some suggestions, but nothing definite. However, on both the Canadian and American sides of the border there were areas suggested in which little lakes could be found which were seldom if ever visited by travelers.

Bearing the good wishes, whispered hints and instructions of those who knew us and came to see us off, we left Winton by launch, towing Buddie behind. This was the way to put the close-in distance back of us most rapidly. We noted Buddie's actions as it trailed along back of that launch, riding the wake. It actually looked joyful, even frivolous, as it skimmed over the waves. The boatman remarked how splendidly our little craft behaved. "It's built right," he commented, and we smiled with pride at the praise of our canoe.

At the end of Falls Lake we were motored over a five-mile portage and deposited, luggage, canoe and all on the spacious shores of Basswood. Here another launch was to have taken us the length of the great lake to give us a start into the wilderness. But this launch was patiently awaiting a vital part which had been sent to the factory for repair. Hence, it was here that our paddling was to begin.

I am not sure who was most affected by the imposing grandeur of Basswood Lake—Giny, Sandy or I.

"Oh, boy! There it is!" said Sandy, stretching his arms high as if waving a greeting to this wilderness he knew and loved so well. "Good old Basswood! It hasn't lost an island. And I know them all!" No, Basswood hadn't lost an island. All six hundred of them were out in those clear, cold waters, and doubtless Sandy did know them all.

"Oh, lovely!" Giny whispered. Our honeymoon had been spent in that country, endearing it to both of us.

There was a background to my enthusiasm in which neither of the other two shared, however. In my childhood, when my nature adventures were limited to an Illinois farm and camping on slow flowing Midwest rivers, this region had gripped my imagination. Rainy Lake, Basswood Lake, Lac La Croix and that great area beyond

the border called Hunter's Island—what food for childish fancy! This was the land of the voyageurs, the intrepid canoemen who had sung, paddled, portaged and battled their way back into this wilderness, carrying on the fur trade long before our nation had earned its stars and stripes. Before my tongue could pronounce *voyageur,* I had prevailed upon my mother to repeat it often for me, for the very sound of the word embodied the carefree, fearless, stalwart character of those men. In fancy I went in their birchbark bateaux. I heard their shouts and their shots. I listened to their songs, set to the rhythm of their strong paddling. I dreamed myself into their rough camps, listened to their coarse, unrestrained laughter, looked upon their fights. I saw bands of Indians—Sioux, Ojibwa, Cree—come to trade, offering skins in exchange for trinkets. To my childish thought theirs was the ideal world in which all was unending romance—a word defined by a voyageur as being "beauty mixed with danger."

A dozen times I had stood at this very point, heading into that wilderness. It was as fresh and thrilling to me now as if this were the first. My voyageurs had sailed among those very islands. Their great canoes, sometimes as much as forty feet in length, had dashed along, each propelled by a dozen skilled paddlers, among the islands upon which we now gazed. On those islands were little bronze posts which at the same time marked the ancient route of the canoe men and set forth the border of the United States and Canada.

"It isn't so much what you see, as what you know is there," Sandy began saying, breaking into my thoughts. "You can't see any more of the wilderness here than we could back at the Sanctuary. But you know that beyond those distant shores are no roads, no towns, no cabins. That makes what you see look even lovelier."

He was right, but I didn't understand how he could talk at a time like that. I just wanted to stand and look and think. There is a feeling comes upon such an occasion which has been described as "having butterflies in your tummy." I knew there were no moths fluttering about in my innards, but it certainly felt like it—and they could have been about the size of crows from the sensation.

Our mood was broken into when an old Indian guide came walking down the trail. We recognized him as

"Indian Joe," well known to travelers of the canoe country. His stride was slow and measured, the pace of woods dwellers; his eyes squinted with the habit of looking long distances, and his bronze face was wrinkled by years. He paused to inspect our stack of luggage. The canoe, which was still overturned on the shore, drew his approval, and he ran his hand over the hull, touching and testing spots where repairs had been made.

"Good!" he said.

I nodded but did not answer. Woodsmen shy at overanxious conversation. Press them, and they close up like the proverbial clam. They must enter talk at the pace and time of their own choosing. I waited, pretending not to be greatly concerned about our visitor, though I wanted to pry into his thoughts and experiences.

The old Indian looked at our packsacks again. He shook his head critically. I knew what was coming. In canoe travel, each one has his own notions about necessities. One will prefer to go extremely light. Another strives for comforts, even luxuries, and takes along loads of supplies. Often the latter works himself almost to exhaustion carrying the things that he thinks make for comfort. Guides of the region like to tell tales of "tenderfeet" who try to carry along mattresses, crates of eggs, bushels of oranges, and of the classic instance of the party that brought along piano rollers to roll their loaded canoe over portages! My preferences put me somewhere in the middle. I do not travel as light as some, but certainly not as heavy as others. However, I take much more than would be in the plans of this Indian who stood before us.

"How long you stay?" he asked.

"'Bout a month," I said, trying to be casual.

"Humph—thought you never come back!" He broke into a narrow smile, designed to indicate humor in his remark. Then his face sobered again.

I said something about taking pictures and needing lots of equipment, but my explanation made no impression upon him. Taking too much equipment is more than just a personal choice in the view of such a man. It violates some sacred frontier laws. No one has any right to be comfortable in canoe travel, or to eat more than barest necessity. There is little room for fussy tastes, none for luxury.

"What this?" Indian Joe asked, delivering a kick that was entirely too strong to a certain case on the ground.

"That is a guitar," I said, feeling terribly guilty about something or other. Perhaps I should have added, "Now, my friend, I am going to carry this. You will never have to lift it once. It is all my job, my muscles, my business. I know that is too much duffel, but it only concerns me. Now please let it and me alone." I couldn't! There is no such thing as your own business in that country. Wilderness travel was this man's life. He knew how it should be done. Maybe he wouldn't turn me over to international courts for violation, but he could make me feel my utter degradation at what I had done.

"You play?" he asked, looking at me from under knit eyebrows.

"Yes."

His expression never changed and he delivered a milder kick to the instrument in question. How could I tell him that no campfire is complete without guitar music? How could I tell him that we didn't travel just to go to some spot in the fastest time, that we looked upon the whole adventure as the object of going. It was as important to have guitar music as food, though surely he wouldn't even have listened to that thought.

I wondered what my punishment would be. It was not long in coming. Slowly the Indian began telling a story, in short staccato sentences. Giny and Sandy drew close to listen. His son, it seems, had gone out on a month's trip over a trap line in the dead of the previous winter. He had frozen his feet, after having gone through the ice in a shallow stream. And the reason he had frozen his feet—this was the point that was to impress us—was that he did not have an extra pair of socks along. "An' I tole him it serve him right!" said the old Indian, with paternal authority. "I tole him when he go out for month in winter he otta take extra pair of socks!"

The old Indian walked away, leaving us to ponder the story and apply its moral to the pile of luggage which, under the circumstances, looked mountainous.

Butterflies were fluttering more furiously within us when we began to pack the canoe. We had spread our too abundant luggage about, the tents at one place, the cameras at another, the packsacks at another. It is necessary to do a carefully planned job at first, until things finally settle into their places.

"Let's not forget anything on this trip," I cautioned, afraid of my own butterflies. "We're sort of excited, you know. We'll need everything we have, whether that Indian thinks so or not. Suppose Giny check on the camera equipment each place, Sandy be responsible for the packsacks and sleeping bags. I'll look after the tents and small articles. At every portage, each one will check up on his own articles."

Fine idea, they agreed. "I'm watching this pack day and night!" said Sandy, indicating the heaviest of the outfit. We shared his concern about that one. In it was a twelve-pound slab of hickory-smoked bacon! Bacon was very scarce in those days, but a camping trip without it was inconceivable. This we had obtained from a farmer who smokes his own meats. Sandy stooped over to smell the smoke scent which made its way even through wrappings and packsack. "Oh, boy!" he said with an out-of-this-world expression. "That is sweeter perfume than roses, lilies and arbutus combined! It would take the Russian Army to get that away from me!" A few days later came an event that caused us to recall that remark.

We were under way now. Much of the day was already gone, and we wanted to reach a certain island in the eastern end of Basswood as a campsite that night. Sandy pulled bow paddle, I was at the stern. I had to caution him about his paddle. He pulled on it so hard I could see it bend. Then Giny and I saw him do something that made us both laugh. We were far out in the lake now, where the water was deep and clean. After a stroke, Sandy raised the blade of his paddle over his head. As the water ran down, he put the edge of the blade in his mouth, and drank several swallows. It was his old stunt of drinking on the lakes, and it warmed our hearts to see it. Sandy was in his wilderness again, and getting more at home every moment.

Our pace quickened. We were still far from our home of the night. A stop must be made at a Canadian Ranger station to obtain the necessary permit for travel. In the southwest a cloud was rising in a threatening manner. Lightening was playing about its caverns and its loose fringes indicated it was riding on a strong wind. It promised the kind of weather one does not wish to face in a canoe.

I always liked to watch Sandy when there was a real canoeing test at hand. He loved the challenge. His smile broadened and his eyes danced. He buried his paddle to the end of the blade, his body entering into each stroke, his long arms working tirelessly, while we could feel the canoe lurch forward before his strength.

We reached our island camp in plenty of time—at least, we thought we did. Sandy and I both remembered every detail about the campsite, an old log which was used as a bench, a rock that served as a table, a level spot for the tents. The first drops of rain were falling as we landed. We were doing all right, but we had to act quickly. The first thing we had to do was put up the tents so we could get our equipment out of the weather.

"Bring up the tents, while I cut some poles," I called to Sandy. Giny covered the camera equipment with our raincoats.

"You must have taken them," called Sandy, as he looked among our baggage.

"Taken what?"

"The tents."

"No, I haven't seen them."

"Neither have I," said Giny.

Then came one of those awful realizations that leave one in a state of absolute helplessness.

"We forgot the tents!" I said. "They are back on that far shore."

"What do you mean, *we* forgot them!" exclaimed Sandy, holding his head in horror. "That was your department, *you* forgot them."

He was right. It was my fault, and mine only. "But it makes no difference where the responsibility rests," I argued. "I may have forgotten them, but we are all going to get wet. Come on, Sandy, you know the old canoe stunt."

He and Giny told me plenty about my carelessness, but they did it on the run. Rain was really coming down. We lifted good old Buddie over to a level spot. Once more the canoe was to serve us. It had that way of fitting into almost any circumstance. We turned it over and placed the most valuable parts of our equipment under the ends. Packsacks were waterproof anyway, so we made sure they were closed tightly and then left them out. The storm broke with unexpected fury. In a few moments whitecaps were racing through the lake. Rain came down in torrents. Giny, Sandy and I crawled under the canoe. We stayed fairly dry, despite the great downpour. Occasionally a little stream of water would flow under the canoe, causing us some discomfort, but in general we were protected. The rain fairly roared on the hull. I was glad, for it made conversation impossible. I knew the ribbing I would take from both Giny and Sandy for my forgetfulness.

That kind of a storm seldom lasts long. This one blew itself out quickly, and as the sun went down there was a great calm over the region. We began cooking dinner and making plans. It was of no use to attempt a trip back for the tents that night. We could sleep in the sleeping bags, and tomorrow make the round trip. It would delay us one full day, but that made no difference now; we were in our canoe country.

Evening came, and with it a campfire. Mosquitoes made themselves felt to some extent, but they are relatively scarce in August, so we ignored them. The much criticized guitar was brought into play and we worked through our repertoire of campfire songs. Our Sanctuary Lake song was repeated several times. There was life to its words now. In the midst of it Sandy's sharp eyes caught sight of something out on the dark waters. "It's a canoe," he said. "Coming this way, too."

The craft was moving along rapidly under expert handling. It came directly to the shore near the campfire, and we recognized one of the two men in it as being our old Indian. The other was his son, we learned—the one who went camping for a month in the winter without a change of socks!

"You take what you no need!" said the old Indian. "You no take what you do need. Why you leave him?"

He held up our two tents for us. He brushed aside our gush of gratitude with some more criticism of our equipment, and then said, "You play?"

We continued our campfire music, the two visitors sitting in silence and so stoically that it was impossible to tell whether they liked what they heard or not. Then we talked with them about the country, the pictures we were making and the little lake we hoped to find. I asked Indian Joe if he knew of such a wild spot.

"No!" That was all he said. He stared into the fire in silence for some time, and then arose to go. Our offer of pay for his thoughtfulness and trouble in bringing the tents was accepted with a grunt. As he was about to leave he walked over to the guitar, now returned to its case. I feared another kick was coming, but he reached down with his hand and patted it the way he had Buddie and said, "Good!"

When they were drawing away from the island into the night, he had to take one last shot at me. "In all my life," he said with meaning, "you first man I see who go camp and forget tent!"

XXI

CHALLENGE IN THE WILDERNESS

IN SPITE of Indian Joe's thoughtful efforts in bringing our tents to us that first night, we did not use them. The night was bristling with wonders from which we did not want to be shut off, not even by the thickness of a canvas. The air had been washed clean by the storm. Stars sparkled dazzlingly. Along the serrated treetops of the distant shore, the brilliant star Capella crept, flashing alternately its red, green and blue-white as if semaphoring a message of hope and happiness.

Sometimes we forget in our habits of living that insulation works both ways. The fine structure of homes that keeps out weather and temperature, keeps us in as well. Seldom can we think beyond our walls. The seething, natural world of winds and wild ways is pictured as a kind of enemy against which we must fortify ourselves. The thicker the walls the greater our protection—but the deeper our confinement. One is nearer to nature in a house than in a great hotel. The separation is thinner still in a tent, where only a layer of cloth lies between us and the universe. Thought can filter through the warp and woof of the canvas and mingle with trees and stars. Sounds can come in. We get within speaking distance of nature in a tent. However, the feeling that we are "a part of all our eyes behold" really comes when all invented dwellings are thrust aside, and we sleep under the star-studded canopy of heaven. The greatest comfort mingled with the greatest volume of natural beauty, to my thought, is a night in a sleeping bag in the wilderness area of the north. Of course, it must be the right kind of night. I am not so hardy that weather and mosquitoes make no difference. Either one can drive me into a tent. But when it is cool, or even cold, and the insect pests are at a minimum, I love to spread my sleeping bag near the fading embers of a campfire, watch the night halfway through and dream it the rest of the way.

Our first night, spent on that little island in Basswood Lake, was the right kind for tentless sleeping. Sandy, so happy that he was silly, took his sleeping bag to the top of a little hill—said he wanted to play with the stars. Several times we went through the *Squoip* routine, much to Giny's discomfort. I asked Sandy if he would be able to sleep in the spot he had chosen. His bed was spread on a rock, and there were humps and bumps beneath him that suggested anything but comfort.

"After the places I have slept, this is like an innerspring mattress," said the soldier. "Besides, I want something to keep me awake for awhile. I want to be sure I am not dreaming."

Giny and I spread our sleeping bags near the fire. We thought we would stay awake, too, listening to the wilderness night and watching the parade in the heavens. But solitude has an anesthesia all its own. Then, too, star dust

CHALLENGE IN THE WILDERNESS

gets in your eyes. I thought I was watching every act of this great nocturnal drama; something happened just as I saw the last flame flicker out in our campfire, and the next thing I saw was the blush of dawn in the east.

There are two firsts that are deeply important on a canoe trip—the first dawn, and the first long portage!

The dawn was glorious. Already color was mounting in the sky as I slipped out of my sleeping bag and dressed. It was cold, but my northwoods clothing was adequate. I walked down to the water's edge. Buddie, the canoe, lay near the shore. It creaked a little as I touched it affectionately. "Buddie, old boy, we're here!" I whispered. "We are in our canoe country again!" The old craft was in its element. It seemed as native to these surroundings as the island and the trees. Here was the old feeling, the companionship, the mutual trust and dependability that make the relationship of a canoeist to his canoe a special kind of friendship. I knew not what problems were before us, but I felt that old canoe, even with its scars of service, was equal to it. And there it lay on the shore, like a bit of visible poetry, adding beauty to the dawn, and giving assurance to the day.

"Beautiful, isn't it?" came a whisper behind me. There stood Sandy, beaming like a full moon.

"When did you get up?" I asked.

"Been up. Been all over the island. I am commencing to believe it—we're up here!" And Sandy looked at the growing dawn as if he would like to eat it up.

Sandy suggested a little canoe trip around the island,

but I bade him go alone for there was something else I wanted to do. I worked my way through shore-line brush, seeking something memory spoke of faintly. It was down near the eastern tip of the island, as I recalled, when years before I had landed on this spot for a short stay. Dawn was brightening somewhat now, and I could see my way. I came to a spot that looked much like what my memory pictured. There was a long flat rock leading down to the water. A tall white pine that looked familiar stood at one side. I walked a bit beyond the tree, quite confident now. I stumbled upon the object I was seeking even before I saw it in the dim light. There was the bronze peg, cemented in the rock, set square with the world, marker of the international boundary. Through the center of this peg ran the line which at the same time separated and yet held together Canada and the United States, a border three thousand miles in length which needed no fortress. I looked toward the east and could see where Basswood Lake narrows down to a simple channel. The boundary line would run through the center of those waters. A short distance beyond that which my eyes could cover would be Prairie Portage. I stood squarely astride the old route of the voyageurs, then. Prairie Portage was known to them as White Wood Portage, Basswood Lake as White Wood Lake, the name commonly in use then for the Basswood tree. Prairie Portage had been an early camping ground. Doubtless overflows of those travelers had used the very island we were on. For there were many coming and going through these waters in those early days. In the early 1800's there were more people entering that region than now.

It did not take much imagination to visualize canoe fleets of voyageurs coming out of the misty dawn. The silence aided the suggestion, and voices of the woods completed the illusion. Just beyond sight could be those carefree, happy, courageous men, a peculiar breed, a nation in themselves. There were debonair Frenchmen, intrepid Englishmen, coonskin-capped frontiersmen, Spaniards, Scandinavians, half-breeds, Indians—all voyageurs infected with the very spirit of the wilderness.

These men loved the dawn. Like the character in Jack London's book, they detested "burning daylight." Dawn was the time to travel, before the winds blew strong and made travel difficult and dangerous. Their campfires were lighted and their camps struck while darkness still gripped the wilderness. They were notoriously happy. Their strength was prodigious. How they gloried in the way they could make a canoe lunge forward and in the great loads they could carry over portages. They were a singing nation. In every gathering someone could be found to play the violin. Songs were sung for the sake of singing. Their carefree hearts must be heard. No doubt the shores of the island on which I now stood, looking and listening into the solitude of dawn, had echoed with their voices. What a sight it would have been to look upon a fleet of their frail birchbark crafts starting out at a time like this, darting through the morning mists, the hardy men stroking to a fast rhythm, laughing, singing, shouting. Had we been there to listen we might have recognized the commanding voice of Alexander Henry the Elder, who had barely escaped the massacre at Fort Mackinac in 1763. These very shores had heard the call of Alexander Mackenzie, Pierre Gaultier, and David Thompson, whose strength, honor, fairness in trading, and Christian character were proverbial in those early days.

It is one of the virtues of dawn that it furnishes such an ideal environment for dreams. Beyond the mists, anything might be true. As the color mounted into the sky and grosbeaks, white-throated sparrows and robins broke into song, I felt the world about me bulging with romance. I could feel the very presence of those characters who had gripped my imagination so firmly since childhood. If I had been let alone I might have solidified some of my dreams. In fact, it seemed as if I had accomplished this. Out of the mists came a real, live, solid canoe, gliding silently along the shore!

For a moment I stared at it in wonderment. It looked like a birch canoe. The lone occupant was tall, strongly built—like a voyageur—and his skill with the paddle was obvious. Had I dreamed a little too hard, and carried myself into a state where my fancies came true? But a voice, coming from the canoe, burst this bubble irreparably.

"Say, I have eaten all the poetry I can digest for now. How about a little plain old bacon?"

A plague on you, Sandy! Who wants to exchange dreams for reality? Why couldn't you have been one of my voyageurs, and gone sailing by from one dream horizon to another?

But Sandy was insistent. "Come on there, fellow, I mean it. I want chow!"

He wasn't alone. Back in the distance I could hear Giny's voice talking along the same line. So I chased my voyageurs away to the eighteenth century and went about the business of building fires, brewing coffee, flipping flapjacks, and broiling bacon. I discovered a little food didn't go bad with me either.

After dawn, Basswood Lake was not a very good place to dream. The evidence of modern trends was too prominent. Launches were passing our island as we packed up. Outboard motorboats plied back and forth with crews of fishermen.

Perhaps I am a crank on the subject, but the sound of motors spoils woods atmosphere for me, though I know they are here to stay and that any objection to them is futile. One of the precious qualities we hoped for at Sanctuary Lake would be no motors. While a motor growls, it is useless for a bird to sing, a squirrel to chatter, a coyote to cry, for no one can hear them anyway.

As Sandy and Giny share my sentiments in this matter, we made haste to break camp and move deeper into the woods. Beyond the first *long* portage we would be reasonably free from these annoyances.

We made a short portage that landed us in beautiful Sunday Lake. We paddled to Whispering Rapids, where a little voicy stream carries the waters of Sunday in small quantities into Burke Lake. Here we had camped several times in years past. The fireplace we once had built of rough stones was there, so was the old log on which we sat before campfires, and the crude little kitchen table where once upon a time I had spilled a can of syrup into a packsack!

Next we reached the long portage. From the far eastern end of Sunday Lake it threads a serpentine course for a mile through highlands and lowlands, over rocks and across swamps, until at last it comes out on Meadow Lake. This trail is a test of any man's endurance, as well as of his enthusiasm for canoe travel. The wilderness seems to have placed it there to turn back the half-hearted. Many there are who enter this country with enthusiasm and progress in great joy until they face this portage. Under sweat and strain of this long carry they feel a sudden yearning for the land of taxicabs, elevators, thick mattresses and luxurious chairs. But if one is so constituted that he can endure and really like the aching shoulders this trail produces; if he can walk over slippery logs and stones, taking the occasional fall which comes his way without losing his disposition; if he can love calling forth the last bit of his strength to climb the final hill, and laugh at the rivers of perspiration that flow down his face and his back; if he can work harder at having a good time than he ever would at making a living, and stand as Sandy did at the far end of the trail, forgetting that the canoe was still on his shoulders, captivated by the beauty of Meadow

Lake—then he is a voyageur and the wilderness takes him into its family!

Giny and I marveled at Sandy. He was aglow with joyous energy when he faced the Sunday-Meadow portage. He knew every foot of it. His eyes flashed as we landed and made our equipment ready for carrying. We must make two complete trips across the trail in order to transport our baggage, a fact that had been seen as disgraceful by old Indian Joe. Sandy seized upon the largest packsack and the canoe. When I objected he was a bit offended. "I've been promising myself this pleasure ever since I left Italy," he declared. "Don't stop me now."

Nothing *could* stop him. He shouldered his load and started out as lightly as if he were carrying a May basket. Down the trail he went, still with breath enough to be singing, "Up along the north horizon, where Aurora's spirits play, there's a lake that rests in solitude, and the wildwood chants its lay." We did not catch up with him until we reached Meadow Lake. There he stood, his selected burdens still on his shoulders, while he looked at the wild shores of the little wilderness lake before him.

"Sandy!" I said, using some of my little bit of remaining breath for laughter. "Why don't you put those things down?"

"Oh, I forgot," said Sandy, unburdening himself.

He suggested that we strike camp right there. He said he remembered something about Meadow Lake. Sandy's memory proved to be good. While we made our tents ready he put out in the canoe, his fly rod in hand. In fifteen minutes he was back with a nice string of smallmouthed bass sufficient for our dinner!

It was a campfire rich in significance that night. We were really in wilderness now. From here on we could actually search for Sanctuary Lake. We stretched our linen map on the ground and looked at it in the light of flickering flames. Sandy was talking. "We'll climb the hills along the shores of Agnes Lake," he said. "You can see miles from there. Maybe we can spot something. Once I got lost in that east arm of Agnes, in those ponds beyond Lake Fouquier. Went up an old dry stream bed and came to a long narrow lake. It looked grand. Wonder if I can find it again."

Our circle grew quiet after a while. We sat looking into the fire for many minutes, each entertaining his own thoughts. Presently it was time for talk again. There is a rhythm to such things. We remarked how fine it was that we tolerated one another's silence.

"If you two approve, I suggest that we tell what we were thinking during that period," I said.

Giny had been thinking of Hi-Bub, wishing that he might be here. She had been reviewing his interest in nature and realizing what it meant in his future happiness. Then she had thought of some of the youngsters we had seen in our travels, little fellows who know nothing but city dirt, city hardness and frustration. She was wishing that more of them could dip into this world of the wilderness.

My thoughts had been prying into the origin of sounds that came floating on the still night air. Some heavy creature swam the narrow width of Meadow Lake, several hundred yards beyond us. Back of us I could hear the rhythmic chewing of a porcupine. There was a cricket calling. In the air about us was the hum of gnats, hanging in clouds a few feet from the ground, a sight that is often thought to be mosquitoes until one learns better. There was the inevitable call of a loon. Surely no wilderness lake would be complete without one.

"And what were you thinking Sandy, you Squoip?" I said to the soldier.

"I was just thanking God that shell didn't get me at Salerno, so I could see this again."

XXII

BEAUTY AND A BEAST

THE next day we moved across a short portage into Agnes Lake. Every modern voyageur probably has a lake he terms "the most beautiful of them all." Lake Agnes certainly bids for that title. It is a long, narrow, deep and clear lake. The shores are mountainous in character. At one place we ran the nose of our canoe against a wall that rose two hundred feet sheer from the water's edge, yet thirty feet from this wall the water was one hundred fifty feet deep. Lake Agnes is not as remote and wild as some of the regional lakes, nor is it on the main route used by the early voyageurs, though it is certain that those inquisitive and adventure-minded men often looked on its lovely shores. Today many canoe parties pass through its rugged grandeur.

Our camp was pitched near the foot of tumbling, singing Louisa Falls. Here the waters of Lake Louisa, the clearest that I know, plunge joyously a hundred feet into the waiting arms of Agnes Lake. The falls make several leaps to complete their journey. On one terrace about halfway down there is a pool and the water coming from above is broken up into moderate spray. This for years has been our shower bath when we have camped near at hand.

We climbed the high rock hills that fringe these shores, and even climbed trees that crest them. With binoculars we searched the rolling, tree-covered country that reached endlessly toward all points of the compass. The forest was studded with jewels of lakes, some of which we could recognize, some we could not. West of us we could see the Silence Lake route, beloved by wilderness travelers. To the east the Fouquier Lake route, leading through beautiful Glacier Lake, passed Little Falls, Koko Falls, Canyon Falls, Kennebas Falls and into Lake Khanipi.

Aside from these known waters, we found little ponds that were without names and that showed only slightly even on aerial maps. To these we made our way, often with considerable difficulty. Few people know how luxurious a cleared trail is until they try to go through the woods without one. To strike right through tangled brush and swamps, over steep, defiant rock ridges, and through blackberry thickets, trying the while to follow a certain compass direction, will raise your respect for the pioneers who first penetrated our wilderness.

Sandy found his dry stream bed leading to the little, narrow lake. It was an adventure to go to it. The footing was difficult as the rocks in the old stream bed were covered with slippery moss. The ancient banks were a jungle of swamp vegetation. We made our way through, a distance of a mile or more, and stood at last on the little lake that had looked like a river on the aerial map. It was beautiful to see. The timber along the shores was mixed, the water clear and deep, and an old campsite was located a short distance from where we emerged. Likely this had once been the home of an early trapper. As we gazed over the land, wondering if this could be the little secluded spot we were seeking, a black bear on the far shore discovered us and raced away frantically climbing the rocky hillside.

Exploration led us to reject the place as Sanctuary Lake, however. There was no evidence of moose, and little about the place to attract them. No lilies were growing in the edge of the lake, no reeds, and there was no swampland. We named this "Not Quite Lake"—not quite what we wanted—and returned to our Agnes Lake camp to plan further exploration.

Another little pond that we found after quite a struggle through the forest appealed to us greatly. It was clear and deep at one end, but had a swampy area at the other, and here we found a great variety of tracks in shore-line mud. There were deer, moose, wolf and lynx tracks, and some that we thought might be panther. There was fine timber on the shores, a place where a good campsite might be made, and no evidence of anyone having been there before us. One thing was lacking. Beavers were nowhere to be found. The proper food was not there. We *must* have beavers at our Sanctuary Lake, so reluctantly we turned our backs on this place. It entered our memories as "Almost Lake."

We always returned to our camp near the falls, tired from these probing expeditions. It was the kind of tiredness that is wholesome and a comfort in itself. We were led to adopt the habits of many of nature's creatures: going to bed and getting up with the sun. Those sleeping bags looked so inviting to us by the close of day that we watched the skies anxiously, waiting for the first stars to appear after sunset as a signal that we could retire.

It was this watching of the skies that brought a kind of calamity on us one evening. We had returned from a strenuous trip. The day was about gone, and we cooked the sort of dinner we could make the fastest. It was bacon and pancakes, the latter having in them a few blueberries that we had gathered. I wish I could get anything to taste as good to me in a city as that simple meal did in the woods! We ate and ate, without counting calories or taking too careful note of manners.

Then our attention was drawn to the western sky, where nature was staging an extravaganza to close the day. Islands of cumulus clouds paused as the evening calm settled on the world. The sun toyed with them. It sent brilliant shafts of light through little openings. It painted the mountainous vapors in scarlet. From northern to southern extremes of the sky the lavish display spread. Voices of the forest exclaimed about the stirring beauty. A flock of crows flew over cawing their loudest. An ovenbird back of us called sharply for "Teacher, teacher, teacher, teacher!" A robin was nearly breaking his little throat with his effort to express himself. The lake mirrored back the loveliness of the heavens. The color grew until the whole world took part in the display. Shore-line trees and hillsides flushed with red. Then it all faded out rapidly, leaving the wilderness hushed and meditative over the grandeur it had experienced.

However, there was *someone* in our camp who was paying little attention to the sunset. We could let ourselves be charmed by its beauties if we wanted to—this was all to his advantage. He moved about seeking something that was far more wonderful to his way of thinking. The pungent odor of a slab of bacon had reached his nostrils, and what could be more heavenly to the practical mind of a bear? We had known the old scamp was around. Bears were plentiful all through that region, and it was not surprising that we had one watching our camp, snatching little food scraps we had placed back in the woods.

There was nothing to fear in the presence of the old fellow. He didn't want to hurt anyone. But packsacks are contraband in his estimation, and he does not count it thievery to take anything he can get. Hence, we had been careful to keep an eye on our supplies, particularly to take them into our tent every night.

Under spell of that grand sunset, we had been careless for a moment. The precious slab of bacon, now about one-fourth gone, lay on a rock where we had been carving it. What a perfect opportunity! The old black rascal must have snickered to himself at the situation. The very least he could hope for generally was that he must rip a packsack to pieces in order to get this delectable food. But here it was laid out for him, and no one to guard it. I imagine it was so easy it made him suspicious. Perhaps he looked and sniffed around to make sure there was no trap. Everything was all right, so he calmly picked up the entire slab, still some nine pounds in weight, and walked away, leaving no payment, thanks, tip or anything.

Right at this moment Sandy turned from his sunset gazing, and looked back at the camp, fifty yards from where we stood.

"Eeyow!" He gave a yell that startled us out of our shoes. "Eeyow! There goes our bacon! Come back here you black so-and-so, or I'll wring your neck."

The black so-and-so didn't come back and his neck wasn't harmed either. He merely raised his nose in the air, waved the bacon proudly and started on the gallop up a hillside. It was a wild scene. Sandy and I took out after old bruin—hopelessly we knew from the start. We shouted and yelled, threw rocks into the brush to frighten him, while Giny laughed until she could hardly stand up. Sandy grabbed the skillet, and as he ran beat on it with a small stick, but the bear ambled on. We could see him at the top of a little ridge now our precious bacon still in his mouth.

Sandy tried pleading. "Listen, funny face, that's our best food. Come back. You can have our sugar. You can have my tent. I'll give you my medal. You can have our shoes. But please don't take our bacon!"

"A-woosh!" went the bear, and he kicked gravel and stones down toward us as he disappeared higher into the hills. Even the FBI and the Air Corps couldn't get that bacon back, and we knew it.

"Come on," said the philosophical Sandy, walking over to the rock where the bacon used to be. "Let's get the last smell from this rock—'cause that's all we're going to get till we go back home!"

XXIII

WAVES AND WOES

BUDDIE was standing the strain so wonderfully we had ceased to think of its frailties. The brace Sandy had put in was holding perfectly. One little patch opened up slightly, but some glue fixed that. We handled the old craft with the respect and consideration to which all canoes are entitled, but which some fail to receive. Once we passed a party who had either little experience in this kind of travel, or little sense of responsibility. They crossed a portage at the same time we did. We saw them drag their canoe up on shore before unloading it, grinding its hull over sand and stones. One of the party stepped in it while lifting out the duffel, and we could hear it literally groan under his weight. When they were ready to embark again, they loaded the canoe fully while it still rested on shore, and then dragged it into the water!

I thought Sandy was going to faint at this display of "barbarity." He bit his lip and withheld comment until the travelers were out of sight, and then he held his head in agony. "It's cruel to use a canoe like that!" he moaned. "It's indecent, it's sacrilegious, it's illegal, it's unconstitutional!" Beyond that, it was dangerous. The party had a strong, canvas canoe; with such treatment they might soon be without one. And my idea of the most embarrassing situation in the world is to be in that country without such a craft. You just couldn't go anywhere, and would have trouble staying where you were. An old guide once said of the canoe, "You handle him like glass." It was good instruction.

The real test of Buddie came unexpectedly one day. We had broken our camp on Agnes Lake, portaged the steep trail beside Louisa Falls, and set our route through the crystal waters of Lake Louisa. It is a big lake, and there was a strong headwind that day. We looked the situation over and decided it was all right to go ahead. The wind was a steady one, not the gusty sort that springs surprises on canoes. It was producing long, even-rolling swells that were challenging, thrilling but not threatening.

We headed right through the middle of this beautiful lake, keeping our bow into the endless legions of waves. The waters were an unbelievable blue, deeper than the sky they reflected. Occasional little wool clouds drifted by, being carded by the winds. Buddie met the waves in sporting manner, climbing over one watery ridge after another. Sandy and I had to paddle with short quick strokes, with never a moment's rest. Our momentum must be maintained. Buddie's bow must stay into that wind and into the waves. If we turned into the trough, the chances of shipping water in our heavily loaded craft were only too good, and swamping was possible.

The wind increased when we had paddled half the length of the lake. We were stroking harder and watching to adjust in a split second any deviation from our course. The situation was really not dangerous, yet it was severe, and a test both of Buddie's stability and our paddling. A large island was directly in our path. We applied extra pressure on our paddles to reach it, thinking to have a few minutes rest in its lee side. Instead, we found ourselves in an unexpectedly difficult problem. The now high waves were divided by the island, and meeting again on the side which we were approaching. The result was a choppy sea which was just about all we cared to endure. Waves came at us from three directions. It was impossible to head into them.

"Wahoo!" shouted Sandy, as a wave broke over the bow and filled his lap with water. "We're in for it. Dig in your paddle there, pal, we have to go places—but quick!"

"Wahoo!" I yelled, catching Sandy's spirit. "We must be men now if we are going to make shore."

It was a grind. We paddled with all our strength and every bit of skill that years of this sort of experience could produce. At first we seemed actually to lose headway. The prancing, sharp-pointed waves tossed us around as if we were driftwood.

I really wondered if we were going to make it. Water was in the canoe, lots of it, and Giny was sitting in it. "Keep calm, dear," I was saying with what breath I could spare. "Remember the packsacks will float, so will the canoe."

Giny flashed a smile back over her shoulder. "There is

never anything to fear except fear," she said calmly. "And we have too much faith to be afraid of that."

Sandy and I seemed to have more strength when she said this, and the waves looked smaller. Sandy gave no thought to the threat of the situation, however. He was watching Buddie perform, with unrestrained admiration. "Look at that old canoe!" he shouted. "Look at him take those waves. Not another canoe in the world would ride them that way. Look at him respond to the paddles. He's a thoroughbred, I tell you. Yea, Buddie! Yea, Buddie!"

We both took up the call of "Yea, Buddie." It set up a rhythm for our paddling. The grand old canoe was behaving magnificently. There was never a wave too quick for it. It dipped water now and then, but was always on top, as irrepressible as a cork. We shouted with delight as the old craft slapped one wave after another with utter defiance.

We were close in now. The waves were higher and more savage. A new problem was included. Barely under the surface were huge rocks, typical of that granite country. To be picked up by a wave and slapped down on one of these things was not to be desired. Once I thought it had happened. A powerful side wave had veered us from our course. Sandy, with his outstanding skill and now at his best, reached far ahead of the bow, and brought us around, co-operating splendidly with my counterstroke in the back. Then we heard the sickening sound of a boulder grinding on the underside of Buddie. For a moment we tipped menacingly. Somewhat aided by another wave we slid off the hidden hazard. There was a severe scratching, a lurch as we straightened away, and we drifted free.

We paddled on, wondering how deep was the scar. Shortly after this we sailed into the calm water, and ran our bow into a short sand beach, the only spot on the entire island where we could have landed. The strain over now, we sat resting, regaining our breath. Then we went ashore, spread our equipment in the sunshine to dry, and with some foreboding turned our canoe upside down to inspect the damage done. It was not as bad as we had feared. There was a deep scratch the length of the hull, but nothing that would weaken the craft. A little more glue and a little more varnish, and Buddie would be as good as ever.

"Oh, boy, what a canoe!" Sandy was saying, throwing his arms around Buddie's bow. "Where would you find another to ride waves like that? You brought us through, Buddie, and I love every sliver in you."

Which may sound a little silly, but you just have to appreciate a canoe like that.

XXIV

BUSY BEAVERS OF MAYBE LAKE

WITH the passing of a few days we had struck the voyageur's stride. Our shoulders were hardened to the feel of portage loads, and our arms equal to paddling without rest. The amount of our exploration and travel each day was limited only by the weather and the hours of daylight. Our campfires had lighted the shores of Khanipi, MacKenzie, Pickerel and Sturgeon Lakes. They flickered on the winding route of the Maligne River. Our songs echoed on little unnamed streams and lakes that our constant searching revealed.

Adventure with native animals was frequent and always thrilling. Animal lore does not grow old. It gains in interest and appeal as our understanding grows.

We saw deer repeatedly, standing in shallows, wading in streams, looking out at us with unveiled curiosity, or racing back through the forest, white tails waving. Never did it become commonplace. The delight Giny and I felt was doubled in watching Sandy. "Oh, boy, did you see that fellow!" he would exclaim, knowing full well we had been watching the buck to which he referred. "Talk about grace—he had more than his share."

On a point of land we saw what might be styled "the cutest" sight in nature. There were a doe and twin fawns.

The two little fellows were having quite a play for themselves. They raced back and forth, hopped over logs in sort of show-off fashion, heads aloof and tails too. At times it looked as if they were playing stump the leader. One would run over a path chosen for its obstacles with bushes, logs, and fallen tree tops in the way. In easy grace

the young creature would clear these barriers in leaps that had much genuine joy mixed in them. The second one would follow the route, proving its ability at this forest game. We could hear Sandy chuckling softly as we drifted along, unnoticed spectators of their play.

Presently the mother doe discovered us. She bounded away a few steps, then halted and looked back at her busy youngsters. They were too preoccupied to notice her. She snorted at them, and at us. Still they paid no heed. She stamped her feet. They merely played the harder, now rearing up and pawing at each other in mock battle. She snorted excitedly, for our canoe was drifting in rather close to shore. The fawns stopped short and stood like statues. Suddenly they spied us, then not over fifty feet away. The look of innocent surprise that came over their faces almost forced us into hysterics. Sandy insisted their mouths fell open. Certainly their eyes could not have become wider unless taken out of the sockets. They decided to run, but didn't know just where to go—so they ran flat into each other. The mother was perplexed. She snorted again and stamped her feet with growing emphasis. The little spotted creatures finally untangled themselves and bounded to their waiting and worried parent. As they went running by, the exasperated old doe reached out with her front foot and planted a one-blow spanking on the rump of her nearest offspring.

Sandy could hardly contain himself. He laughed until the canoe shook, though maybe, as Giny suggested, Buddie was doing a little laughing himself. "Boy, oh boy, wasn't that cute?" exclaimed Sandy, using a word you would hardly expect of an embattled veteran. "That was worth every portage we've made. Did you ever see a neater spanking dealt out in your life? Bet he'll learn to obey orders now—maybe!"

In one narrow river, its course half filled with basket grass and lilypads, we noticed a bear cub, about six months old, just entering the edge of the water. Apparently he thought he was the only living thing in that whole region. He paused and drank a little in the shallows, so sure of his safety he did not even look around.

"He's thirsty," whispered Sandy. "Bet he's been eating our bacon his daddy brought to him."

However, we were many miles from the campsite where our bacon had been stolen. Young bruin waded deeper into the water and still unmindful of us began to swim. Of course, we had ceased paddling and Buddie was drifting splendidly in that characteristic silent way. On came the bear toward the middle of the stream while we sailed along with the current. We could hear him giving little snorts to clear his nostrils of water. Still he showed no caution. Whose wilderness was this, anyway? Is not his kind, the black bear, king of the woods? Who would dare threaten him, and bring forth the ire of his all-powerful clan?

The whole maneuver was timed perfectly. Destiny was written on one little watery spot of that river. There we met: the venturesome and reckless baby bear and Buddie with its cargo. The nose of the little creature had almost touched the canoe, when lo! he discovered us. I remember when I found a bee in my breeches; I can remember finding a porcupine in my bed; I remember Giny finding a mouse in her slippers—but I never saw more excitement in any living thing than when baby bruin awakened to the presence of that canoe! The astonishment of the twin fawns was mild in comparison. The little black fellow beat the water about him into a lather. He tried to go every direction except down. With the wildest flurry of paws, he succeeded in whirling about and starting back to the shore from which he had come. He left a wake behind him like that from a launch. Lilypads were cast to the four winds. All the while he was giving out little squeals like those of a young pig, to which animal he is related. Out through the woods he went, leaving a trail of squeaks behind him, no doubt seeking a big, powerful mother who was capable of giving the required comfort and protection. We journeyed on, but not until we had recovered from our laughter sufficiently to use a paddle.

One precious adventure was mine alone, the gift of a little lake we found far back in a range of tree-covered hills. The lake itself was entrancing. It was so nearly what we were seeking that even when we left we were undecided, and thought we might return there. Hence we named it "Maybe Lake."

Giny and Sandy had climbed a little hill to get a view about the country, while I circled the lake shore. The shore was the only disappointing thing about the lake. It was muddy all around. This was due to beaver dams at the outlet. The whole region bore record of these animals. Fresh cuttings were everywhere. Logs newly peeled of bark were floating in the water. Shore trees and brush were flooded. There was indication of moose, deer, bear, and other creatures in runways that I found. But this was a beaver paradise, unquestionably.

At one point I heard a sound that made me proceed with caution. It was the gnawing of a beaver. Apparently these animals were so undisturbed that they worked in broad daylight, something they would not do when people invaded their realm.

Presently I discovered the worker. It was a good-sized one, weighing perhaps sixty pounds. I watched it from back of a towering red pine for several minutes. The beaver is a wary creature. While this one chewed at a fallen tree, laboriously cutting up the log into lengths suitable for handling, it kept on the alert. Presently it detected me, perhaps by sight, or maybe some forest breeze carried my scent to the animal. Into the water it went, and immediately began warning the world that danger was near by slapping the water in resounding smacks with its tail.

I laughed a little at the commotion, but immediately I was silenced by another sound. Up on the high land away from the lake and directly above me there was something stirring about in the leaves. I watched closely. Soon appeared four young beavers, lusty kittens, still new at the forest game. I walked right out in front of them. They paused about ten feet away, puzzled but apparently not frightened. Down in the lake the old creature, which I now realized was the mother, splashed about more frantically than ever. She was right in the edge of the water looking anxiously toward the little ones. I walked up to the young animals and they made but slight effort to avoid me. One I was able to pick up, and holding him in such a way that he didn't "unbark" me the way he would a tree, I looked him over. He seemed quite contented and made no effort to free himself. He was a beauty, chubby and healthy. His soft brown fur was a joy to see and to touch.

The mother was not so complacent as her kittens. Her actions quickly drew my admiration and my sympathy. She floundered about in the water, trying to divert my attention. She pretended she had been hurt, and floated helplessly on her back. She came out on shore and dragged herself along trying to convince me that she could not escape if I wanted to trade the one I held for her. When I did not respond, she became more bold and insistent. She inched her way over the ground toward me, crawling after the manner sometimes employed by a dog who is desperately soliciting forgiveness from his master. I was so struck with her devotion and courage I could hardly let the drama continue. But I held to my hostage, knowing that though it might mean temporary discomfort for her, no harm was really coming to her youngster. The other three had now entered the water. Finally this devoted salf-sacrificing mother came within three feet of me, and there prostrated herself on the ground—a willing sacrifice for the liberty of her young! I could stand it no longer. I placed the tiny fellow on the ground, and the two of them scampered to the safety of deep waters.

This experience was told and retold during the rest of

the day. It was the subject of campfire conversation that night. In fact, it was almost a deciding factor in convincing us that we had found our wilderness paradise. But there were some things just a little short of our hopes, so we journeyed on promising that we would return—maybe!

XXV

THE GUITAR MAKES A CONQUEST

THE busy days trooped by all too fast. Our strenuous program of travel was interrupted occasionally by bad weather, but there was not as much time used this way as we had anticipated. Anyway, a rainy day now and then is a great convenience, yes, even a blessing. Sometimes you get tired in this world and do not know what is the matter with you. You become disinterested in what is happening, grouchy, irritable, and all that is really the matter is that you are tired.

The story is told of some travelers in the South American jungles, who were moving along at a forced pace. The native guides and packers were driven to the utmost. One day the explorer, a white man of international fame, came from his tent ready to renew the hurried journey. But in place of the usual industry, his packers sat on their haunches not making a move to get ready. All the threatening and pleading he could employ did not stir them. Their explanation was that they were going to wait for their souls to catch up with them. They had the hurried sense that was creating confusion in their minds. The peace of well-timed action was gone. They were not going farther until that feeling of peace came again. Furthermore, their leader knew that they were right!

Our rainy days kept us from a similar error. The several we spent in our tent with the rain crooning a monotone melody on the thin canvas were a special kind of joy. There were problems about our cooking, of course, but problems are purposeful because they offer the opportunity for triumph.

Always there was reading to do. Into our overstuffed packsacks I had forced several small volumes especially chosen, another bit of luggage that would have drawn criticism from Indian Joe had he known it. But like our guitar, these were more than worth the extra lifting. Our minds were ready to receive great thoughts in such surroundings. One's wealth in this world is measured by his thinking.

It seemed to Giny and me that we would rather have toted a hundred books across those portages than to have missed one particular experience with Sandy. The rain was beating furiously against the tent, and it had been the day of our longest confinement. The forest was soaking wet, like a fresh-dipped sponge. Buddie lay overturned across two logs, as much water washing over its hull as if it were sailing in the lake. We reclined against our bedding rolls, passing the wet hours reading, talking and occasionally singing a few songs. Sandy had Emerson's *Essays,* a book that I insist will accompany me no matter where I go. Giny was reading the *Bible,* while I had another volume rich in revelation.

"May I interrupt?" asked Sandy.

We put down our books and listened.

"Boy, this hits me right between the eyes," said the soldier. "Ralph Waldo was certainly hep. Listen to this: 'There is a time in every man's education when he arrives at the conviction that envy is ignorance—'" the soldier was pointing to the lines as he read—"'that imitation is suicide; that he must take himself for better, or for worse, as his portion....' Boy! That's good stuff!" Sandy was all stirred and animated by the words he was reading.

"'That though the wide universe is full of good,'" I went on, quoting from memory words I have known since boyhood, "'no kernel of nourishing corn can come to him but through his toil bestowed upon that plot of ground which is given him to till.'"

"You know that by heart?" said Sandy.

"Indeed I do—by heart!" I emphasized the last word. "I wish everyone in the world would take that right into his heart."

"And here!" Sandy went on enthusiastically. "Wonder if he wrote this just for me.... 'The power which is in him is new in nature, and none but he knows what that is which he can do, nor does he know until he has tried.' Doesn't that sort of tell you to mind your own business?"

"Yes, it does," I laughed. "And it tells you that your own business is worth minding. It is your business and belongs to no one else. Minding it is a duty, a privilege and the only way you will find happiness or satisfying success."

Sandy became silent, thinking. The rain increased in volume, huge drops making a tom-tom of the tent. Our soldier rolled over into a new position and prepared to search more deeply into the volume that had stimulated him so much.

"Then," he said, half to himself, "a fellow doesn't need to feel ashamed if he's different so long as he is *himself*—and minds his own business!"

"Certainly not," said I, joining in a conversation I wasn't sure was meant for me. "He need only be different in the finest, most honest way he can."

"Remember those words from 'America the Beautiful'?" asked Giny—and she quoted, "Till all success be nobleness and every gain divine." Then she continued, "Whatever work a person does in life, his success really is rated by the character he has developed."

Sandy's eyes narrowed with thought. Then with a comprehending smile and a meaningful wink, he plunged into his book again.

Fair days multiplied our adventures rapidly. We worked the length of Lake Kahshahpiwi, over the exasperating portage to Yum Yum Lake, and peered into the country thereabout. We searched the region of Sarah Lake, and found it thickly populated with moose. For a brief instant we saw a lynx early one morning on the shore of Basswood River. He was at the edge of the water, possibly fishing for his breakfast. He discovered us almost at the exact instant we saw him, and vanished with the marvelous quickness of his kind.

On mighty Lac La Croix, whose bays are spread out like a giant cross, we floated for a while before the mysterious

Picure Rock. There were animal forms, tracks, and Indian symbols drawn high on the face of a cliff by bronze-skinned artists centuries ago. On wandering Crooked Lake we looked upon another art gallery of ancient origin. Here on rugged walls of granite some unknown genius of the tribes who peopled this area had drawn in vermilion figures of many animals of the region. High above these drawings was a great vegetation-filled crack in the cliff, which was often referred to by the voyageurs. In their day, many arrows were seen sticking in this crack. The origin of these arrows is not certain. One story tells that they were left after a battle between the Sioux, plains Indians who occasionally invaded this region, and the Chippewa or woods Indians who lived there. Another account says that this was once a test of marksmanship, and that young men of the Chippewa were required to prove their skill with the bow and arrow in this manner. Now only the yawning crack remains, glorified by the tradition.

Our adventure chest was being filled to the brim with golden nuggets of experience. Yet, we had not found our Sanctuary Lake. There were a number of near misses. But each one fell short of the high and exacting ideal we had formed. We commenced to think that we were expecting too much. We wondered if the seeking of our little lake was not all there was to it, for certainly it had been grand just to go prying so energetically into this region.

Our time was running out. There was still vast territory to the north, east and west of us, into which we had not entered. Indeed it would take a lifetime to investigate every nook and corner of this great region. Now our campfire conversations had begun to refer to going home, an idea we did not wholly like, and yet there was an appeal to it. On two occasions we met parties headed out of the canoe country. Through their courtesy we sent letters to be mailed, one in each case addressed to Hi-Bub. His parents told us later he almost lived on those letters, reading them and having them read over and over again.

One marvelous evening we camped at one end of a long portage. The moon had been growing in size until now like a great mellow arc light it flooded the forest land. Islands visible from our campsite seemed to move about as if the moonlight had severed their anchorage. Our campfire looked tiny and insignificant, like the flicker of a birthday candle in this vastness. This was an evening for music. We played and sang for a long time. Sandy had a new verse for our canoe song, and we all learned it:

> We have followed trails and portages
> Of the Chippewa and Sioux,
> We have ridden foaming rapids
> And faced strong head winds, too.
> Still we seek that little wildwood lake
> To whose shores our hearts have gone.
> It is somewhere east of sunset
> And it's somewhere west of dawn.

This superb wilderness night called for periods of silence, too. There were moments when singing was silenced, and we three sat listening to the rhythmic throb of the forest. The portage on which we were camped had its romantic background. Companies of voyageurs had made their way through here to and from the far west, laboring, sweating, singing under their heavy cargoes. The ancient trail led back from our campfire, disappearing in a veil of mist as trails do in moonlight. Such moments seem timeless, and I felt as if an Indian might appear out of those soft, filmy shades. I glanced up to the trail—and there stood an Indian!—not in feathers and primitive regalia, to be sure, but an Indian just the same.

"Joe!" I said, startling everyone with my voice. "Don't do that to us. That's quite a shock."

Indian Joe grunted some kind of a hello, and came on toward the fire, followed by two very pleasant men who were laughing and apologizing for their intrusion. We invited them to join us about the fire. The three, we learned, were camped at the far end of the portage. Joe was guide for the party. His keen ears had caught the strains of the guitar and so he had led them over the forest trail to hear the music. They had been standing in the shadows for some time listening before I chanced to notice them.

"You play more?" asked Joe, pointing to the guitar which lay in my lap.

"Sure I will," I said, delighted that our critic was finding the instrument was not excess baggage after all.

In a few minutes our visitors were joining in our songs, and an atmosphere of friendly good will reigned that was as grand as the moonlit night itself.

When singing had subsided, Giny and I engaged Joe's two companions in conversation. They were interesting, knew people we knew and had been many places we had been. But I had difficulty in keeping my attention on our conversation. There was something going on between Sandy and Joe at the far side of the fire. My ears reached frantically in that direction but they heard only enough to stir curiosity up to the bursting point. I heard Joe say something about "lake," and then our own conversation filled my ears. I saw Sandy excitedly fire questions at Joe, and the Indian reply with more sign language than words.

Now Joe began drawing a map in the sand! "Yes," Sandy said enthusiastically in a moment when our talk had died down, "I remember that. Why didn't I think of it before?"

THE GUITAR MAKES A CONQUEST

Our talk went on, and theirs did too. Sandy went to the tent and got a map. He and Joe tapped it with pointing fingers as they talked on. I nearly popped.

Our visitors took their leave early. The next day would be a busy day for us all. As they were leaving, Joe stooped down and patted the guitar. "Good!" he said, with more enthusiasm than I had ever seen him show before. "I like him! You always bring him, huh?"

"Certainly, Joe," I said. "Whenever you find me in the canoe country, the guitar will be there too."

"Good!" said Joe, and then he added in a way that let me understand what he had done was out of appreciation of that guitar. "I tell boy sumpin'."

Yes, he had told Sandy "sumpin',"—and I couldn't get it out of the Squoip! I begged and coaxed and threatened, but Sandy wouldn't talk. "Don't you trust me?" he asked repeatedly as if offended.

"Yes, I trust you, Sandy, but can't you tell me why you went and got that map, and what you two were talking about?"

"Never mind. If you trust me, be ready at dawn. We have places to go and things to do."

We were ready at dawn. Sandy knew something but, darn his hide, he wouldn't tell a thing!

XXVI

THE SECRET OF INDIAN JOE

WE TRAVELED hard all one day from the portage where we had met Indian Joe and his party. We traveled just as hard for part of the next day, and then came to a small bay along the shore of a very large lake. There appeared to be very little to mark the place, but Sandy was satisfied. He insisted we camp there for the night. We would need a full day for what was before us, he said, and it would be unwise to start with just an afternoon at our disposal. We teased him constantly to tell us what we were doing, but he didn't weaken. All we could get out of him were those same words, now repeated with exaggerated emphasis and weird gestures, "Don't you trust me?"

"Yes, Sandy, you low-down Squoip, we trust you," I said helplessly. "What else can we do? If we drowned you, as we want to, your secret would be forever lost. Lead on, Squoip, but remember, someday when this is all over, we'll sit down to dinner and not tell you it's ready!"

Next morning we were packed up and set to go by the time the sun peeked over the horizon. Sandy found a faintly marked trail leading back from the shore, a discovery which caused him to show much joy.

"But, Sandy, that is an animal runway," I said, protesting against unnecessary labor. "That doesn't lead anywhere that we want to go."

"Don't you trust me?" asked Sandy, sinking to his knees before me.

"Oh, phooey!" I said, shouldering my packsack and starting down the trail.

The animal runway wound through the forest for over a half-mile. It followed a ridge, and then cut down through an alder thicket into a valley. Here we found a little pond, with rather muddy margins. Apparently it was part of an old stream that one time had been connected with the large lake we had left behind. Likely the waters were now finding their way toward the sea by a subterranean route. The stream reached on back into the hills, too, for we could see an ancient channel now choked with grasses, lilypads and reeds.

"Sandy," I said, showing the strain I was under, "this is nothing but a mud puddle! We can't waste our time here. Be reasonable——"

"Don't you trust—?" he started to say, but I let out a yell of agony.

"OK, I trust you!" I said, resignedly. "Go on, lead us into quick sand. Take us back where even a mosquito can't go. We have nothing to do except make mud pies. Go on, we trust you!"

We loaded the canoe, and with some difficulty put off from shore. The banks were extremely soft, and we had to bring forth a log from which we could embark. We had not gone far when we reached the grass-filled channel. There were several inches of water present, but the vegetation was so heavy we could make no progress with our paddling alone.

Of necessity, we originated a system of locomotion that took us along at a rate of about fifty feet every five minutes. We would dig our paddles into the muddy bottom, and calling in unison, "Umph!" literally jerk the canoe along by lurching forward with our weight. "Umph!" "Umph!" "Umph!" ran the concerted command, as poor old Buddie was forced through the reeds, as abused as any canoe that ever floated. Since then this little stretch of clogged stream has been called "The River of Ten Thousand Umphs!" And I think the number is not an exaggeration.

Presently the going was a bit improved. We came to a beaver dam, much to Sandy's delight. Apparently he had been looking for just this. We lifted our equipment over the dam, paddled a little distance up the pond, and came to another dam. There was another, and another, until we had crossed seven of these dams, each in fine repair, giving evidence of a large, active beaver population. The ponds were muddy, of course, and the forest flooded by them. But beyond the last one, we came to a clear, flowing stream. Around several bends of this little river we paddled, now terribly excited. Then we came to still water! We rested on our paddles, simply entranced at what we saw! A marvelous little lake lay before us, walled in by high granite cliffs. The water was clear, cold and obviously very deep. In area, the lake would be smaller than the one on which we lived in Wisconsin. But it had that wilderness charm that made us fall in love with it at first sight. At the far end there was a deer drinking, and we looked upon the graceful creature as a messenger sent to greet us. The shore was low at this point, and there were lilypads aplenty. "Grand for moose," I remarked,

and Giny added, "There is one now!" We were passing a narrow point, and in the bay that unfolded to view stood a magnificent bull, his antlers probably five and a half feet from tip to tip. We chuckled with delight as the old forest monarch fled along the shore, weaving his great head between trees and through brush.

There was one saddening note working its way into

our happiness, however. Giny had noticed some water on the bottom of the canoe. At first we thought it the draining of paddles, but we saw the volume was too great for that. Investigation proved it was a bad leak. The River of Ten Thousand Umphs had been too much for Buddie. Both bow and stern seams had opened a little. The wood itself was decayed, and repairs would be difficult. Like our packsacks, our spirits were considerably dampened at the discovery. We were drifting rather far on the worry side, when a cry of delight came from Sandy, making us forget temporarily this new problem.

"There!" He was looking up toward a tall cliff. "That is what I have been watching for. Look up on those rocks."

We looked in the direction he was pointing. There was a low cliff of granite, the face of which was covered with dark lichens. In this had been scratched in poor script the letters "J O E."

"This is it!" shouted Sandy, now releasing his enthusiasm. "The old campsite must be just around that point."

The old campsite was, and we landed there. It was on a nice flat area, bedded deeply with a deposit of pine needles, the gift through the years of the great red and white pines that grace the shore.

Then we got the story. Joe had come here years ago and established a sort of private fishing ground of his own. The lake was filled with bass, a fact which we proved by dinnertime that night. He had never guided parties to this place. This was his own. He wanted the animals undisturbed, wanted them so he could talk with them and live with them. Joe no longer wanted to kill his brothers of the forest. His love for them was too deep for that. He regarded them as his companions in wilderness life. To this little lake he had come when he wanted to be alone. "To talk with God," he had said to Sandy. It was his Sanctuary Lake. But now his years were many. He might not come there again. He wanted us to know where it was, for he told Sandy, "People who sing, play and not kill—they good!" Sandy remembered seeing the animal runway on that lakeshore years ago. Once he had followed it to the pond, but he went no farther. Hence he knew what Joe was talking about that night before the campfire. He promised we would never disturb or destroy anything in Joe's Sanctuary.

Now we made camp, our hearts singing. Even though we had not investigated the lake, we felt that it was the one of our dreams. A bit of exploring added to this feeling. There were moose, deer and beavers—we had already learned that. Unmistakable signs of bear were soon found, and there was an animal runway near the lowland that seemed to contain every kind of track possible in that country.

Across from our campsite, there was a great tall dead tree in the top of which was an osprey's nest. As we approached it, two large adult birds took to wing, circling above us and screaming wildly. We soon discovered the cause of their excitement. A sizable youngster climbed up on the side of the nest and looked down at us. His appearance was the signal for his parents to scream louder than ever. They dipped low over our heads, seeking to divert our attention from the young one. They flew at him and actually beat him with their wings to make him get down. But not that young fellow. He had never seen such funny-looking animals before as those who walked around on the ground gazing up at him, and he meant to watch them. Finally one of the parent birds came flying along carrying a good-sized fish in its talons. The older creature flew directly over the nest, dipped low, and dropped the fish inside. It was bribery, but it worked. The youngster got down off his perch on the side of the nest, and probably indulged in a feast.

Evening came, and with it conviction that this was the Sanctuary Lake we sought. Dinner, consisting of freshly caught bass, was out of the way and for a while we sat before the campfire. There would be little sleeping done that night, we knew. Excitement ran too high. Together we composed the last verse of our canoe song:

> Now our campfire glows upon the shore
> Of our Sanctuary Lake.
> If you seek our forest paradise,
> Here's the only trail to take:
> Pack along the north horizon
> In the home of goose and swan.
> It is somewhere east of sunset
> And it's somewhere west of dawn.

Then we went canoeing! Giny paddled bow that night and Sandy stern, for regardless of canoe leaks, I must sit in the center, guitar in hand. The great cliff where

Joe's name was carved echoed back our strumming and songs.

We kept no account of hours. The moon climbed to the zenith, flooding the wilderness with its cool light. Stars peeked timidly down, but the moonglow was so great only Capella and Vega could show to advantage.

Now came an adventure so rich in poetic beauty we could scarcely believe it real. It was as though the wilderness had been saving this experience to crown our trip. Some way we had qualified for the best. Perhaps it was because we had not let ourselves become discouraged. We had played the game of wilderness travel fairly. We had guarded our campfires, we had kept the places clean where we dwelt, we had taken from the waters only what we needed, we had destroyed nothing, wasted nothing.

Whatever earned us the reward which was now before us, we were grateful. We had reached the extreme end of the lake for the first time. It was in the small hours of the morning and the moon was at its best. Here we found a slender falls leaping a few feet into Sanctuary Lake, its water looking like molten silver in the moonlight. This seemed enough of a miracle in itself. We had hoped our lake might have a waterfall, but we would have been satisfied with less. Yet there it was, seeming to flow out of the night itself, chanting an old, old story as it entered the lovely lake. We drifted silently, watching this epic of beauty.

There was an animal moving the brush.

"A deer!" whispered Giny.

Yes, it was a deer, but it was one in a hundred thousand. At first, had we believed in such things, we would have mistaken it for a ghost. It was conspicuous even in the shadows, and when it walked fully into the moonlight we realized that we were seeing a pure albino! It looked as if it were the very moonlight incarnate. The lovely creature moved toward the dainty waterfall. It was the poetic thing for him to do, and he seemed to know it. He bent his beautiful head to drink, while the silvery stream flashed and flowed in the moonlight.

Nothing could be added to make the picture lovelier. We shall never forget a single detail of that exquisite scene. The feeling of wilderness, the serene waters on which we floated, the graceful canoe, the moonlight that flooded the nocturnal landscape and the fairylike creature before us completed a divine display that sank deeply into our hearts.

Brevity is part of such supreme beauty. The great white buck broke the spell when he tossed his antlers high and then made his way into the brush, drawing the shades of night behind him.

"Let's go back to camp," said Giny, the first one who found voice. "I couldn't stand it to see another miracle tonight. This is *it,* all right. Only Sanctuary Lake could present a scene like that!"

Yes, this was it. This was the lake of our seeking, that had begun as a dream, lived as a promise and now was a reality of experience.

"How about a little gab fest, Sam?" asked Sandy as we strolled down to the lake shore in front of our tents, just before retiring.

"Nothing I would rather do, Sandy."

"Are you glad you trusted me?"

"Yes, you Squoip. But it seems to me that we would have come here just the same even if you had shared the secret."

Sandy wasn't listening, though. He was looking up at the heavens. More stars were breaking through the moonlight, as that queen of the night skies crept toward the western horizon.

"There is order—divine order—in all this, isn't there?"

"Yes, Sandy."

"Everything is in its right place, isn't it? Everything fits—is that true?"

"Yes, that is true."

"Then everything is created to be right where it is, made for that purpose. Nothing can get out of place, can it? And everything has to do the thing it was meant to do, doesn't it?"

"Yes, Sandy." I loved the trend of his comments, and quoted briefly from a beloved hymn, "'In beauty, grandeur, order, His handiwork is seen!'"

"That's the idea," exclaimed Sandy, enthusiastically. "This natural universe is like a jigsaw puzzle, it all fits together even though all the pieces are different. Now, why isn't that true of men, too?"

I nodded my approval.

"What I mean is, everyone fits where he does his best. Take Indian Joe—he does a fine service to people. He's giving those men something that will help them always. And look what he gave us? But he's just himself, doing what he can do the best he can, minding his own business."

I waited for Sandy's next statements. The boy was thinking clearly.

"Well, I'm not afraid of civilian life any more," he said firmly. "The power that keeps those stars in place has a place for me, too. If Joe can serve, so humbly and yet so well, I can too. And I can do it in my own way."

We stood in silence again for a minute. "Do you feel more sure of what that way is, Sandy?" I asked.

"Yes, I do. Don't you suppose there are a lot of other people in this world who want to find their own little Sanctuary Lakes? Oh, I don't mean exactly the way we have done, but they need to get into solitude and find themselves. There must be a right place for them to do it. Wouldn't I be serving to help guide them back in here, kind of pointing out the way to enjoy nature, and maybe sharing some of the ideas you and I have talked over? Wouldn't that be a service?"

"It sure would, Sandy."

"Then if that is natural to me, isn't it being as great as a salesman, or an engineer, a businessman or a lawyer?"

"Most certainly it is."

"All right, you are talking to Sandy the Squoip, guide extraordinary in the canoe country. If I can't handle all the guiding myself, I will hire others to help me. But here I am going to live and to work. Ralph Waldo says I must take myself for better or worse, and I'm ready to do it."

We shook hands. Had I no other evidence than Sandy's clear thinking to prove to me that we had arrived at the lake of our dreams, this was sufficient. A person must stand on holy ground to realize, as Sandy did, that in himself are the talents and the opportunities through which he must work out his salvation. Not in the world, but in his own character is his work. Success is not measured by comparing himself with his neighbor, but rather in the degree he cultivates and uses his natural ability.

"Sandy, my boy," I said as we walked slowly toward our tents. "Maybe some of those you guide will be lads like yourself, standing between school and the business world, feeling lost and bewildered. Perhaps you can lead them to stand for a moment in silence, listening not to human advice, but rather to the wisdom of the ages within their own thoughts. He who does that learns that he is dear to the heart of the Creator, that his talents are new to the world and that he has a high purpose to perform. Wherever this realization came would be a wilderness sanctuary as prized to the one who experienced it as this lake is to us."

"I have exactly that in mind!" said Sandy.

The first gray streaks of dawn were in the sky before I closed my eyes in sleep. I wanted to review the miracle of our experience, fasten its every detail in my thought and make it mine by prayer of gratitude. For nothing **is fully** possessed until gratitude is expressed.

XXVII

MEMORIES AND MANNA

SEPTEMBER was in its prime when Giny and I were once more living at our island home in Wisconsin. The place seemed dearer to us than ever before. The now distant Sanctuary Lake had taken nothing from this precious cabin. Each was an original love in itself.

We were in the midst of the autumn carnival. Oaks, aspens, elms, sumacs, birches stood in indescribable array. Hillsides flamed with color, as though the rainbow had showered them with its priceless hues. Shore lines fairly sang with brilliance, and in quiet hours the lakes multiplied the startling scenes in reflections.

The long evenings were ideal for memories, and we devoted them to this purpose. We had so many wonderful things to recall. What a vast vault memory must be to take in such a volume of experiences and still offer room for as much more.

For two days we had stayed at our newly found wilderness retreat. Every foot of the shore line was explored, and we pried into the country back of it. In every way it surpassed our expectations, as reality always does.

Sandy had devoted his time mostly to repairing the canoe. This work was no longer a mere enthusiasm, it was profoundly necessary. That canoe was the frail connecting link between ourselves and the outside world. We had to go home in Buddie, or it was possible we wouldn't go home at all. The leaks were truly serious. Until now it had been rather easy to put on a patch, or fill a hole with glue, or varnish over scratches. But with the seams opening at bow and stern, the problem was much more severe. The wood itself would not hold. Sandy was resourceful and skillful with the repairs, but the job when finished did not give us absolute assurance. Buddie was literally laced together with rawhide bootlaces, aided by glue and varnish, supplemented by balsam sap. The result kept us pleading with the old canoe, "Just last until we get out of here, Buddie old boy, don't let us down."

Buddie made good. The old canoe was faithful to the end. We reached Winton, the little town where our car had been left, still afloat but that was all. The rawhide was pulling out, the glue and balsam sap inadequate. Giny was sitting in water and our luggage floating as we finished the journey. Buddie seemed to give a groan of relief as we lifted him out of the water and placed him on the top of our car. Certainly, the three of us sighed our gratitude.

We bade Sandy good-by as we left him at his home. From reports it seemed certain that he was near the end of his military career. He smiled now, as he spoke of the coming civilian life. No longer did it frighten him. The faith and understanding that had dawned on him at Sanctuary Lake prevailed. Once I asked him how he felt about it all. He replied, "I know that if God can govern the universe, He won't have any trouble steering me around so long as I am willing to be steered."

At the island there were many interesting things awaiting us. Hi-Bub had done a wonderful job, bless his heart. He nearly exploded when he saw us. There was so much to tell he was trying to relate three stories at once. His family had taken a house in town and Hi-Bub was knee-deep in school. Saturdays and Sundays he could make trips out to the island, so that made the rest of the week endurable. He was worried about the woodchucks, though. He hadn't seen them since September 10. Then he saw only one, and that for just a moment. It was Patty Sausage that he saw, he believed. Patty and all of them got so fat they could roll faster than they could run. On this day Patty was peeking out of a hole in the ground. It was quite cold, and a strong north wind was blowing. Patty seemed not to like it. He didn't respond to the coaxing of Hi-Bub or his daddy, but just stared around. Not even a carrot would tempt him to come out. Finally he disappeared slowly into the ground.

"No doubt he went to sleep, Hi-Bub," I said, for the woodchuck is our longest hibernator, and it is not uncommon for him to enter his deep sleep before the middle of September.

It took quite a little explaining to make our boy feel comfortable about the woodchucks. He was all for shouting into their holes until they came out and got something to eat. I told him that the layers of fat he had noticed on the little creatures would nourish them through the winter, but he wasn't exactly convinced. He couldn't think of that as being a very good way to absorb food. To chew and taste things was a better idea. However, by the time he had shouted himself hoarse trying to get the "Thauthage" family to come out, he concluded that maybe he had better let nature take its course.

Hi-Bub drank in every word about the finding of Sanctuary Lake. His imagination ran rampant. He had it pictured with waters of gold, with animals sitting around in droves. I fear his schooling suffered through it. From what was told me I gathered that no matter what class was in order—spelling, arithmetic, reading or what—he talked about Sanctuary Lake. And some of the stories made mighty good listening if you had a sense of humor, his teacher said.

Gradually we checked up on the Sanctuary animals. Ratzy-Watzy had vanished. Likely the constant tormenting by the squirrels was more than he could stand. We were glad he left of his own choice. Another development pleased us too. Racket, the little raccoon that had first appeared in such unhappy condition one day in early summer, was quite normal now. His coat was thick and dark. Furthermore, he had been taken into a family, either his own or one that adopted him. A fine-looking large female raccoon came to our feeding station nightly guarding and guiding four lusty-looking youngsters, one of which was Racket. We rather favor the idea that this was his original family. Raccoon mothers are not so ready to adopt orphans, according to our observations. Of course, this leaves a lot of explaining to do. We asked ourselves questions we could not answer. Had his mother directed him to our island originally, with the idea that it was the safest place for him in his condition? Or had he made his way alone, and finally by accident was reunited with her? Much mystery must remain about this experience, but this is true: the little fellow came to the best place in all that country in which he could recuperate. My inclination, after years of observation, is never to charge anything to chance in nature. It is all cause and effect. Intelligence, often of a higher order than what we call reasoning, guides the people of the forest. As a rule, I believe the best thing happens that could happen under each circumstance.

We returned in time to see an amusing climax in the conflict between No-Mo and the island squirrels. He had not abandoned his plan to return to that original home. No doubt there had been continuous arguing going on. Hi-Bub said that whenever he came he found squirrels chasing each other. No-Mo won a complete victory. He not only earned the right to return to the island, he caused More-Mo some way or other to share the attic with him. We realized that this had happened when we found the two squirrels actually playing together. More-Mo had accepted the companionship of the other. And really there was nothing else he could do! No-Mo would not be denied.

More-Mo held something in reserve. His trust was not

absolute. No-Mo could share the living quarters if he insisted, but not that great store of food that More-Mo had assembled with such labor. One morning we heard a persistent pattering of feet overhead. Upon investigation we found out what was going on. More-Mo was carrying every nut, seed, mushroom, pine cone, and piece of dry bread he had stored aloft, out into the forest, hiding them in various places. No-Mo looked on unconcerned. Apparently this was all in the agreement. Where No-Mo's store of food was I did not know, but obviously More-Mo was not going to divide his. He did share it in spite of himself, however. The blue jays had a field day. That business of carrying food into an attic had been too much for their thieving habits. There was nothing they could do about it. Now the conditions were more to their liking. More-Mo buried some peanuts under leaves and in shallow pits. Some he placed on rafters under the shed, some in chosen spots in trees. Each place selected was easy for the sharp-eyed blue jays. I don't know what percentage of the treasure they pilfered, but it was plenty. More-Mo innocently worked on, probably thinking himself a very wealthy squirrel, though now his possessions were not as great as he supposed.

One other adventure with these squirrels is well worth relating. We noted that the crop of pine cones was far below normal. Likewise the other seeds of the forest were less than usual—the acorns, hickory nuts, hazel nuts, etc. Hence, the food of such creatures as squirrels and chipmunks was greatly reduced. It was a serious problem.

The little fellows sat around apparently not knowing just what to do. At this season they should have been busy storing things constantly, but there was nothing to work on. On the mainland the problem was not so severe as those animals could roam farther in search of food. But we felt responsible for the creatures who dwelt on the island. There were too many of them for such a small area anyway, and no doubt we had induced them to stay by aiding them with their provisions. We must make good on our obligation to them. The peanuts we had contributed had been limited in quantity, as we did not want the animals to depend wholly upon this imported food. Hence only enough had been given out to keep them looking to us for part of their supplies.

Now with winter coming, something should be done for them. Accordingly, Hi-Bub and I went searching for squirrel food. It was discouraging, but we finally assembled half a bushel of acorns. To this we added a similar amount of peanuts. Then one morning we decided to scatter this about, and let the squirrels work at storing it.

The chickarees had formed the habit of running up to the cabin whenever the door slammed. Usually all four of them would sit there a few feet apart, scolding each other, and begging us. One peanut would be tossed to each, and away the creatures would go.

On this particular morning came the deluge. The squirrels came running up as Hi-Bub and I emerged with our bushel basket of mixed nuts. The four creatures sat begging and scolding as usual. Instead of one peanut each being tossed out, it began raining nuts. Hi-Bub and I took handful after handful and tossed them high in the air. The squirrels stopped scolding. They looked at each other in blank amazement. Peanuts fell beside them; they couldn't pick up one. Acorns fell under their noses; they were unable to take a single bite. Whoever heard of such a thing? The sky was opening up and flooding the earth with food. It was simply incomprehensible. One peanut each they could understand, but not hundreds of them! What were they to do?

Hi-Bub had the time of his life. He loved to feed animals anyway, and this chance of smothering them in food was perfect. He laughed and giggled while he tossed handful after handful into the air, making a little jump each time he threw. Still the squirrels just sat and watched. Then they started making the silliest little chirps, which were probably the red squirrel for "Wow!"

It was many minutes before they were able to stir themselves. Then they ran from one nut to another digging little holes hurriedly and burying each one *right where they found it.* I expect in the entire history of their kind there have never been four other chickarees so utterly dumfounded as were these the day manna fell from heaven in quantities beyond calculation.

XXVIII

A CANOE IN THE SKIES

THE first snowstorms were visiting the north country, even though the echo of summer had hardly died away. Winter was practicing, and the result was beauty extraordinary. Before the trees had lost their color, fluffy white flakes settled upon them. Leaves of orange, crimson and maroon held little handfuls of cottonlike snow as though startled and proud at the beautiful effect. It did not last long, for the sun was still strong, but while it was there the scene was exquisite.

Between autumn and winter is a period of sharp contrasts. For several days the temperature held at fifteen above zero. All growing things became thoroughly chilled. Then there was a sudden change. A southern wind, warm and moist, blew into the region. When it touched the cold twigs, plants and trees, it left a generous deposit of frost on each one. The result to the countryside was dazzling. Every little twig, every pine needle, every blade of grass was white and glistening. It looked as if the northland had been silver-plated. Even delicate little spider webs were frost covered, looking like silver threads. Giny and I ran out of adjectives. When beauty reaches such heights there isn't really anything to say—you just have to look and love.

Our mail had been bringing us happy bits of news. Sandy was in military camp again, but it was certain that his discharge was not far away. Word came that Bobby, the boy mentioned in earlier writings, was safe and well when fighting had ceased. So was the fine boy I had introduced in a previous book as Duke, and his companion Lieutenant Still-Mo.

The day was nearing when we would leave the Sanctuary for our winter's work. One pressing problem had not been solved as yet. In fact, I was avoiding it as long as possible. It had to be faced, and I realized the time had come one day when Giny said in serious voice, "Sam!"

"Yes?" I knew what was coming.

"What are you going to do with Buddie? You know something has to be done. If you just leave it here, your sentiment will get the better of your judgment and you will start using it again. It simply isn't safe, and you know you should dispose of it."

Yes, I knew that. There was no doubt that something final should be done with the old canoe. It was through, beyond recall. It had served its purpose in our lives, even to the finding of Sanctuary Lake, but there was no way to repair it further.

I had cast about for ideas as to what I should do with it. I just couldn't chop into it with an ax and make kindling wood of it. That was not fitting fate for such a grand old craft. I didn't like the idea of casting it to one side and letting it slowly decay either.

The disposal of the old canoe became quite a neighborhood problem. One man suggested I make a flower bed out of it, and I had a hard time even to be courteous to him. Make a flower bed of my canoe? Put a lot of dirt and gravel into that craft that had sailed wilderness waters through the years? Impossible! That would be all right for a rowboat, but not for that canoe!

Another suggestion from a well-intentioned friend was that I fill it with rocks and sink it to the bottom of the lake. This put a strain on our friendship. Buddie, that had been the master of waters, now to be conquered by them, and slowly go to pieces among clams and weeds? Inconceivable! There must be a way more fitting than that.

Then came Hi-Bub to the rescue. He was having his first training in the local pack of Cub Scouts. He loved old Buddie, and he had an idea that appealed.

"Tham, you know how you do with an old American flag?" he asked. His lisping was disappearing, and though I know this was desired, I disliked to see it go.

I told him my education in such matters had been neglected—I didn't know just what to do with an old American flag! Would I put it in the rag bag? he asked, tempting me. No, I knew better than that. Would I throw it out on a trash pile? No, I wouldn't do that either. Both methods were decidedly disrespectful. Then he told me what he had learned. When the flag is faded and torn and no longer fit for display, he said, it should be folded very carefully, and then with much respect, placed into a fire and the flames be allowed to consume it.

"I understand what you mean, Bub," I said. "You think

if that is good enough for the flag of our country, it is good enough for Buddie, too. I like it! Buddie is not going to be pushed aside and allowed to decay like ordinary wood. He is going up in smoke in a special ceremonial fire!"

The event was planned for a certain Sunday near the end of our northwoods sojourn. Hi-Bub and his parents came out to the island as did other neighbors. Sandy had been notified, and he sent this comment to be read at the ceremonies: "I only hope I can be as good a man as old Buddie has been a canoe."

We built a roaring campfire in a clear space where no trees could be harmed by the flames. We placed an old packsack and an old paddle in Buddie. We pointed the bow toward the north, then two of us picked up the old craft and laid it in the fire. The seasoned wood caught quickly. In a moment it was a mass of flames. Smoke arose to the treetops and circled on toward the stars. We stood and sang our canoe song. Giny surprised us with a new verse which she had composed for the occasion.

> Paddle on, old Buddie, paddle on
> To a new lake in the stars,
> Where there are no rocks to scratch your sides
> And no logs nor hidden bars.
> We'll look up to you each night and day
> When the rainbow spans the skies,
> For we know that hull of yours is made
> Of the stuff that never dies.

So the old craft passed on into memories. The campfire slowly flickered out. When our guests rose to go home there was only a bed of fine ashes. Hi-Bub gave the comment that was needed. He looked at the ashes on the ground meditatively for a moment and then said, "Boy, oh, Boy! Didn't Buddie burn up thwell?"

Yes, Buddie had burned up *swell*. Even the last act of the old craft was commendable.

There will be other canoes in our experience. After all, it is not so much *a* canoe that we love as *the* canoe. We will find one that is attuned to solitude, that has the spirit of the wilderness. We will give it a name and one day take it over secret paths to Sanctuary Lake.

But there will never be a craft draw more of our love or deserve it more than good old Buddie!

"I'll thay tho!" said Hi-Bub.

SANCTUARY LAKE SONG

(To The Marines' Hymn)

Up along the north horizon,
Where Aurora's searchlights play,
There's a lake that rests in solitude
And the wildwood chants its lay.
In the land of bears and beavers,
In the haunt of doe and fawn,
It is somewhere east of sunset
And it's somewhere west of dawn.

So come, you merry voyageurs,
With your paddles and bateaux,
To the land of sky-blue waters
Where the north-bound rivers flow.
We will search the wide-flung wilderness
For the lake where peace lives on.
It is somewhere east of sunset
And it's somewhere west of dawn.

We have followed trails and portages
Of the Chippewa and Sioux,
We have ridden foaming rapids
And faced strong head winds, too.
Still we seek that little wildwood lake
To whose shores our hearts have gone.
It is somewhere east of sunset
And it's somewhere west of dawn.

Now our campfire glows upon the shore
Of our Sanctuary Lake.
If you seek our forest paradise,
Here's the only route to take:
Pack along the north horizon
In the home of goose and swan.
It is somewhere east of sunset
And it's somewhere west of dawn.